KT-527-355

Managing behaviour and motivating students in further education

Susan Wallace

Learning Matters

WANDSWORTH LIBRARY SERVICE

501339681

The author would like to acknowledge the help of all those teachers and students in further education colleges who participated in the research projects that underpin the information in this book, and to thank Isabella Wallace for her input and feedback on some of these ideas and strategies.

First published in 2002 by Learning Matters Ltd.

Reprinted in 2003

All rights reserved. No part of this publication may be reproduced, stored in a retrieval system, or transmitted in any form or by any means, electronic, mechanical, phototcopying, recording, or otherwise, without prior permission in writing of Learning Matters.

© Susan Wallace

British Library Cataloguing in Publication Data
A CIP record for this book is available from the British Library.

ISBN 1 903300 49 5

Cover design by Topics – The Creative Partnership
Project management by Deer Park Productions
Typeset by Pantek Arts Ltd., Maidstone, Kent
Printed and bound in Great Britain by Bell & Bain Ltd., Glasgow

Learning Matters Ltd
33 Southernhay East
Exeter EX1 1NX
Tel: 01392 215560
Email: info@learningmatters.co.uk
www.learningmatters.co.uk

Managing behaviour and motivating students in further education

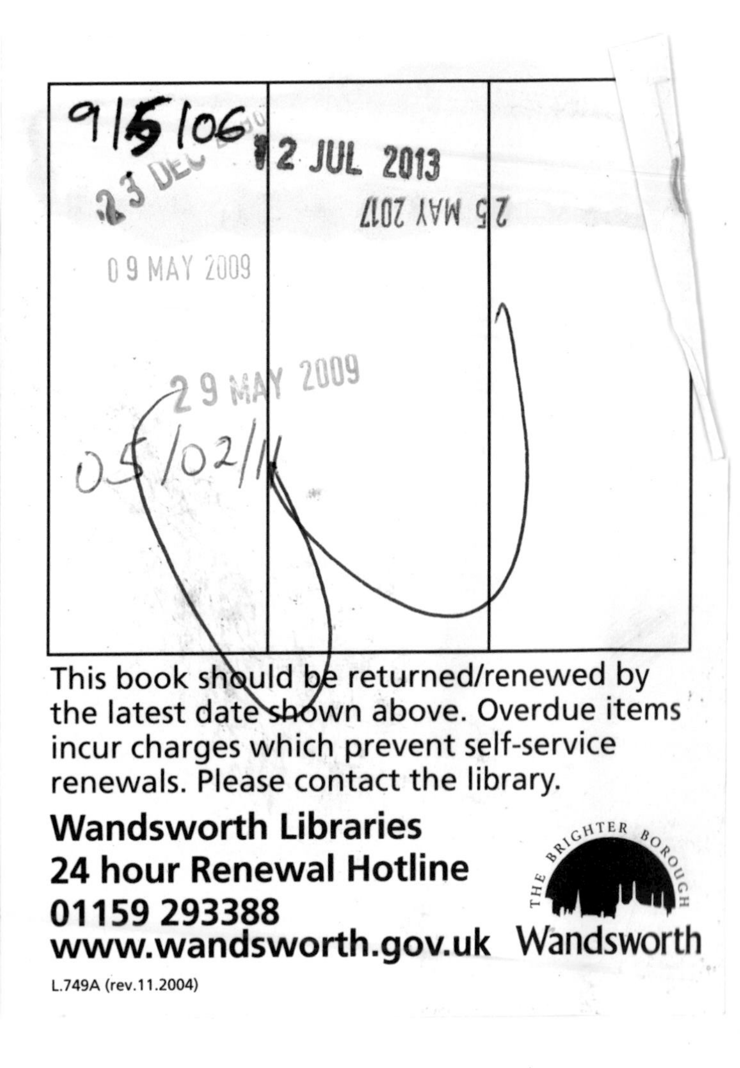
9/5/06
23 DEC
12 JUL 2013
25 MAY 2017
09 MAY 2009
29 MAY 2009
05/02/11
This book should be returned/renewed by the latest date shown above. Overdue items incur charges which prevent self-service renewals. Please contact the library.
Wandsworth Libraries
24 hour Renewal Hotline
01159 293388
www.wandsworth.gov.uk
THE BRIGHTER BOROUGH
Wandsworth
L.749A (rev.11.2004)

501 339 681

Titles for Further Education teachers

Teaching and Supporting Learning in Further Education
Susan Wallace
ISBN: 1903300 28 2
£15

Managing Behaviour and Motivating Students in Further Education
Susan Wallace
ISBN: 1903300 49 5
£12

Teaching Using Information and Learning Technology in Further Education
Chris Hill
ISBN: 1903300 99 1
£14

Please order from our website, www.learningmatters.co.uk, or from our distributors:

BEBC Distribution
Albion Close
Parkstone
Poole
BH12 3LL

Tel: 0845 230 9000
Email: learningmatters@bebc.co.uk

CONTENTS

1 INTRODUCTION

When aspiring Further Education (FE) lecturers come to be interviewed for a place on a programme of initial teacher training, they are often asked the question: 'Why FE? Having decided to be a teacher, why have you chosen this particular sector?' More often than not the answer goes something like this: 'Because the students want to be there. They *have* to be at school; but in the post-compulsory sector they're older and they're there because they want to be. I want to teach students who want to learn. If I was teaching in a school I'd have to be coping with discipline problems, and that's not what I want.' At this point the interviewer will, it's to be hoped, take the opportunity to explain some of the realities of teaching in FE in the 21st century.

Yet these candidates' idealism seems based on a sound enough premise. Further Education is not compulsory. Why would students be there if they didn't want to be? Why should FE not be full of well-motivated students, willing and even eager to learn? These are questions which are unpacked and addressed in detail in Chapter 1 of this book. Chapter 2 offers an opportunity to look at what some of these students themselves have to say about their motives and their behaviour. The remaining chapters look at practical strategies which FE teachers can use in order to motivate students and to establish parameters of acceptable behaviour.

The intention of this book is to address the immediate needs of the FE teacher by providing advice and ideas of a practical and sometimes pragmatic nature; and also to show where these relate to recent and current learning theory. This is not a theoretical book. It is based very firmly on what teachers and students in FE have to say about their experiences. It draws on the findings of three research projects into student behaviour in FE. One focused on the experiences and perceptions of student teachers new to the sector; one looked at ways in which more experienced teachers defined and managed difficult student behaviour; and the third focused directly on the students themselves, and the accounts they gave of their experiences, their behaviour and their motivation. What these lecturers and students have to say can be found in detail in Chapters 1, 2 and 8. Sometimes what they have to say contradicts certain areas of accepted theory, and where this is the case the reader is encouraged to reflect upon the contradiction in the light of their own practice. The book is by no means claiming that theory is not useful. Rather, it is making the point that, as professionals, we can only judge the worth of theory when we have measured it against our own experience; when it has been, as Keats puts it: 'proved upon our pulses.' As professionals reflecting on our practice we may do our own theorising, and indeed should be encouraged to do so.

The book is designed to meet the needs of the teacher at all stages of their professional development. Each chapter is clearly referenced to the FENTO (Further Education National Training Organisation) Standards for Teaching and Supporting Learning in FE (2001). These standards will continue to bear their original name.

The content of each chapter in this book can be used for professional development by teachers who are working towards Stage 1, Stage 2, Stage 3, Postgraduate Certificate of Education or the Certificate of Further Education; and by fully-qualified and experienced teachers whose continuing professional development would benefit from an exploration of issues around student behaviour and motivation. It presupposes that the teacher, at any stage of their professional development, will be keeping a journal in which they reflect on their professional practice. It also presupposes that they will have access to support within their institution or place of study, from a mentor, tutor or colleague who can act as a critical friend. This emphasis on reflective practice is in line with the requirements of the FENTO Standards. More detailed, practical guidance on how to keep a reflective journal in this context and use it as a basis for planning future practice can be found in Wallace (2001) *Teaching and Supporting Learning in Further Education: Meeting the FENTO Standards*. Readers with little prior experience of FE, or whose experiences have been limited to a narrow range – for example, student teachers, or teachers working towards Stage 1 – may find it useful to reflect in their journal on scenarios and dilemmas contained in these chapters, in order to extend the scope of their reflection.

The book uses case studies, dialogue and extracts from FE teachers' journal entries in order to explore these key issues of student behaviour and motivation. Taken together, these represent, I hope, an accurate and realistic account of some of the more difficult aspects of the FE teacher's role. The reader is asked to engage with the material; to analyse and reflect and offer suggestions for future practice. In this sense, too, the book supports the model of the reflective professional.

Chapter 1, as we have already seen, addresses the question of why student motivation and behaviour have become such an issue in FE. It argues that an understanding of the possible causes which may underlie challenging behaviour will help the teacher to identify effective strategies for dealing with it. In doing so, it seeks to provide a social, historical and theoretical context for the chapters which follow. Some readers may wish to begin with one of the more practical chapters, and turn to the more contextual, theoretical material in Chapter 1 as and when they feel the need to reflect on some of the wider issues which form the background to their classroom practice.

The practical focus of the book begins at Chapter 2, 'Students talking', which looks at what students themselves have to say about why they are in FE and what motivates them to remain there. This is based on one of the research projects mentioned earlier and draws on the responses of fifty students of all ages and levels of ability. They speak about their previous experiences of education and training and how these have shaped their attitudes. The chapter encourages the reader to analyse and reflect on these accounts, and draw conclusions for their own planning and teaching.

Chapter 3, 'Where do we start?', is about identifying the student's starting point, and using it. It suggests ways in which the teacher can find and build upon what is positive and also on what simply is. In the process it examines how students may be motivated by challenging and modifying their often negative construct of 'the teacher'. Chapter 4, 'The Rule Book', looks at establishing rules for appropriate behaviour in order that learning may take place. It suggests ways in which appropriate behaviour can be agreed and monitored, and it examines the disadvantages of having too many or too few rules, or of enforcing them too rigidly.

Chapter 5, 'Great expectations', is about how our expectations of our students, and their own expectations of themselves, can influence their ability and willingness to learn. It suggests ways in which the teacher can raise students' self-esteem and help them to set positive, achievable goals. Chapter 6, 'Breaking out', encourages teachers to think outside the box. It illustrates and discusses the usefulness and limitations of various theories of learning in relation to motivating students and encouraging positive behaviour, and encourages teachers to recognise and evaluate their own personal theories of learning.

Chapter 7, 'Putting the flags out', looks at ways teachers can help students to recognise their own achievements, however small. It is about finding successes to celebrate, providing a positive role model, and giving positive and constructive feedback even in the most difficult circumstances. Chapter 8, 'Teachers talking', relates in teachers' own words some of the most difficult or confrontational incidents they have had to deal with. It draws on the research mentioned earlier into the responses of one hundred FE teachers. The strategies they have used are analysed and evaluated in order to present the reader with a range of possible solutions to difficult situations.

There are recurring themes which run through all these chapters. They include strategies for appearing confident and in control; ways to counter student preconceptions about 'The Teacher'; and methods of establishing workable parameters of acceptable behaviour. The main argument of this book is that student motivation and appropriate behaviour are prerequisites for effective teaching and learning, and that to address either of these issues we have to know something about our students as learners. Getting to know our students, raising motivation and establishing parameters of appropriate behaviour: the chapters which follow aim to help the FE teacher to feel more confident about all three of these key aspects of their role.

2 WHY ARE THEY HERE? THE ISSUES OF STUDENT MOTIVATION AND BEHAVIOUR IN FE

Boredom is just 'What's the use?' in disguise.
Julia Cameron, 1994

This chapter addresses the question of why student motivation and behaviour have become such an issue in FE colleges over the last decade. It argues that this cannot be attributed simply to standards of teaching, and that the causes must lie largely outside the classroom. In setting out this argument it seeks to provide a social, philosophical and theoretical context for the chapters which follow.

The material in this chapter may be used for developing and reinforcing the following areas of skills and knowledge as set out in the FENTO Standards.

→ g1; g2; g3; h1; h2.

Choosing to be in FE

As we saw in the introduction, there is an assumption among many new recruits to the FE teaching profession that the students they will encounter in colleges will be willing and enthusiastic learners. The expression often used is that that FE students 'are there because they want to be there'. This is a perfectly reasonable assumption to make, of course, since we are talking here about a sector which is post-compulsory. No-one is forced to be there. Therefore every student enrolled at the college will be there out of choice. Won't they?

Well, of course, many of them will, and many of them will be a delight to teach. They are there because they want to learn and they have found that learning is rewarding, either because it leads to the qualifications they need, or as an end in itself. However, a surprising number of students will not be like this; they will appear uninterested, uncommitted, even resentful; they will arrive late for lessons, or not at all; they will not complete coursework unless endlessly chased up about it, and sometimes not even then. They will be challenging, confrontational, disengaged and unmotivated; they will send and receive phone calls and text messages in class; they'll wander about the classroom or workshop disturbing those who are working; they'll use offensive language; and worse.

All of this may sound extreme or exaggerated; but anyone who has taught in FE recently will recognise some of these student behaviours as part of the FE teacher's everyday experience. To teachers new to the sector, however, this comes as something of a shock. Of forty-one trainee FE teachers questioned about their experience of sitting in on FE classes for the first time, every single one reported in their reflective journal that they had witnessed student behaviour of this kind (Wallace, 2002). We'll go on to look at some of their responses to it as this chapter progresses.

But why should such lack of motivation and such challenging behaviour be so prevalent in FE when, as we have said, students only enter post-compulsory education out of choice? I think the answer lies with that very word 'choice'. It's a slippery word, by which I mean that it may be used or understood in a way that does not quite reflect its real meaning. If we look back over the final decade of the twentieth century and the first few years of the twenty-first, we'll find the word 'choice' used a great deal in the debates over education and training. In 1995, Gillian Shephard, then Secretary of State for Education, told cabinet colleagues:

> *We must emphasise the words that people find attractive, such as standards, discipline, and* choice. [my emphasis].

Unfortunately, when this was quoted in *The Guardian* (15.9.95 p. 6), a misprint caused the list of desirable words to read, 'standards, discipline, and chaos.' As well as causing us to smile, this misprint may also make us stop and think. It may even nudge us into considering the ways in which the language we use about education and training has begun to dislocate some words from their original sense. How much real choice do students have at the end of their Year 11 in school? Or, to look at it another way, how many of them have a real choice at all? And might some categories of students perhaps have rather less choice than others? So when we hear the word 'choice' used in the context of post-16 education, we should also remember Lewis Carroll's Humpty Dumpty, who declared that 'A word means just what I choose it to mean' (*Alice Through the Looking Glass*, Chapter 6). If 'choice' might sometimes actually mean 'not very much choice at all', then perhaps we can begin to understand why *chaos* occasionally occurs in some classrooms.

We shouldn't assume, therefore that negative student attitude and lack of student motivation in FE are necessarily caused by poor standards of teaching. Certainly it often falls to the individual teacher to come up with ways of dealing with the symptoms of this malaise – and that's why this book has been written. But that is not the same thing as saying that there's something wrong with current standards of teaching in FE, nor that 'fixing' the standard of teaching in FE will at the same time 'fix' this malaise. However, understanding the range of reasons behind some students' unwillingness to cooperate may make it easier for us, as teachers, to find more effective ways to encourage and support their learning.

Lack of choice about being there at all is just one possible cause of confrontational student behaviour, and one that we shall examine more closely in the following pages of this chapter. But there are other possible explanations, too, which we will need to consider. Since Socrates, philosophers have been asking themselves this question: 'Why do human beings behave badly?' In more recent times, sociologists have begun to ask – and offer answers to – the same question. And psychologists, some of whose ideas will be illustrated in the chapters which follow, have come up with theories about what might motivate or demotivate us or drive us to behave aggressively. There is, therefore, a huge literature on these issues of behaviour and motivation. But in a practical sense it is only of value to us if it works; that is, if we can draw on our understanding of it in order to be more effective in teaching and supporting the learning of our students. This chapter takes the opportunity to present some of these ideas from sociology, philosophy and psychology in order to establish where our starting point might be. When we are considering how best to motivate a student or to manage their behaviour, it helps us enormously to have an idea of the possible reasons *why* they are behaving in this or that particular way. The student will not always be able to tell us; the reasons may not always be easy to articulate; but having some possible reasons in mind will help us to avoid falling into the trap of adopting a deficiency model of the student. This term – deficiency model – is an important one for us, as teachers, to watch out for. What it means, in our current context, is that students behave in that way because there is something wrong with them, something lacking; in other words, that they are somehow deficient. We have to watch out for it because it represents a rather lazy way out. We can recognise it in ideas such as 'That student is just a bad student. There's nothing I can do about it.' In moments when our confidence as teachers is flagging, we might find we are applying the deficiency model to ourselves, and telling ourselves that the students are badly behaved and unmotivated because we are somehow deficient as a teacher. It is a central argument of this book that a deficiency model of students (or teachers) is rarely helpful as an explanation, particularly when our aim is to raise motivation or standards of behaviour. Other explanations can be helpful, however, in providing a context for our interaction with students, and it is some of these we shall proceed to look at now.

At the same time as we are considering these issues, however, we must not lose sight of the fact that our classes will also include many able and well-motivated students who have made an informed choice to undertake their current programme of learning in an FE college. Teaching in FE is an enjoyable, challenging and rewarding experience. If it were not, why would so many dedicated teachers choose this sector? In focusing on the problems and seeking for answers and solutions, we must not allow ourselves to demonise the sector nor stereotype its students. We should also remember that not all 'difficult' students are sixteen-year-olds. Plenty of adults can exhibit challenging behaviour, as we shall see in the chapters which follow.

Demotivated by lack of choice

We all know from our own experience that a feeling of control over our own lives – a feeling that we have some degree of choice about what we do – is necessary for our sense of well-being; without it we may easily begin to feel discouraged and disengaged. And so in this respect Gillian Shephard is right, of course. We do like the word 'choice', particularly when we are thinking about our education or that of our children. Ball (1993), however, analyses the contradiction around the word 'choice', arguing that current policies may restrict rather than extend the choice of students and parents because, in effect, power of choice – that is, which students or pupils go where – often lies now with the institution rather than with the individual. Schools will usually choose which students stay on to continue their education in the sixth form, for example. So let's consider for a moment exactly how much choice the 16-year-old who enters FE actually has.

At the end of their Year 11 in compulsory education, the choice faced by most 16-year-olds is whether to stay on at school or to continue their education and training in a Sixth Form College or College of FE. Employment is simply not a realistic option any longer for this age group; and even schemes such as new apprenticeships involve some element of college attendance. So, does the student stay on at school or go to college? Or does she drop out altogether, thus becoming ineligible for any financial support? Assuming she does not drop out, then how does she make her choice between school and college? In Chapter 2 we'll read some explanations from students themselves about how they came to enter FE, and why. To judge by these, some of those who enter FE make that choice based on their unwillingness or ineligibility to stay on at school rather than on their preference for FE or for a particular curriculum area. With some exceptions, the underlying principle seems to be this: that students who don't like school, or haven't succeeded at school, or both, will choose to continue their education or training in FE. Students who feel comfortable in school will stay on there if the school's curriculum provides the subjects they wish to study. And if the school chooses to have them, of course.

There are two factors operating here. One is that young people who would in the past have chosen to go into employment now may find that their only option, apart from staying on at school, is to go into FE. This is one of the consequences of widening participation. If we widen participation without addressing motivation, we end up with a lot of participants who aren't necessarily enthusiastic or willing. Moreover, students who choose FE rather than school because they didn't enjoy or succeed at school will include those whose experiences of the education system have taught them to resist and fear it. These particular students could be in your FE class because they disliked school, not because they wanted to be in FE.

How do we restore these students' sense of agency? How do we give them back some degree of choice? There are several suggestions in the chapters which follow, including strategies for negotiation and confidence building.

Vocational courses: giving students a sense of purpose

If students are enrolling in FE because they were not encouraged by their school to enter the sixth form, their achievement at Key Stage 4 is likely to be lower than four grade Cs at GCSE. If this is the case, their choice of FE programme will be limited to those at Intermediate level or below. Such 'vocational' courses, despite the name, are not likely to lead immediately to employment. Most students will have to undertake further study or training at Advanced level in order to gain a qualification which will begin to open employers' doors. Sadly, this can result in students who do not find education rewarding in itself being recruited onto vocational courses with no very great hope of entry to that vocation at the end of it. This again helps us to understand why they can often appear unmotivated, and why their disappointment and frustration sometimes spills over into unacceptable and challenging behaviour. It remains for us as teachers, then, to give them some sense of purpose; to help them to plan for longer term goals and find ways to help them recognise that there is a reward to be gained in the process of learning itself.

Motivation and the employer-led curriculum

Some have argued, however, that this last point itself presents us with a real difficulty (e.g. Reeves, 1995), and that it's the dominance of the work-related qualifications system and its very nature which may be making the FE curriculum less rewarding and less stimulating for younger students. Of course, the curriculum of FE has always been a predominantly vocational one; but it is sometimes argued that the instrumental, competence-based structures of the NVQ (and later the GNVQ) framework, which have been introduced relatively recently, have had the effect of reducing learning to repetitions and rehearsals of work-related tasks and skills. Because many youngsters expect to find the workplace routine mundane and unenjoyable, they respond with the same lack of enthusiasm to the simulated workplace tasks of vocational courses. And added to this, it is argued, there seems to be an acceptance implicit within our current post-16 qualification system that education or training are not rewarding in themselves, but that it is only the qualification at the end that counts. Reeves expresses this neatly as reward by 'accreditation, not by gratification' (1995, p. 105).

This is a particularly interesting theory to consider since the green paper, *Extending Opportunities, Raising Standards* (DfES, 2002) presents the argument that young people disenchanted with school would be better motivated if given access to work-based courses and real work environments. If this proves anything it is that for every theory there is a counter-theory! For us as teachers, however, it is a reminder to think of ways in which we can make learning more gratifying – more enjoyable as an end in itself – and less dependent on the idea of simply mirroring the workplace.

The status of vocational education and training and students' self-esteem

We all know from our own experience, as well as from our reading, that our level of self-esteem plays a key role in determining our behaviour and our degree of motivation. There is – and we shall explore in this section how it has arisen – a perception of FE as somehow being a second-best option. It is quite clear, and again we shall hear this from students themselves in Chapter 2, that there exists a cynicism amongst some students about what FE is for. We have seen how some might view the sector as simply an extension of their compulsory schooling or, at best a holding station. This idea of post-16 education and training as a means of providing temporary occupation for those who will find no place in the workforce is not a new one. It was an accusation aimed at the youth training schemes of the 1980s (Finn, 1987) as well as at the policies for increased participation of the late 1990s (Ainley and Bailey, 1997). Such a commonly held and frequently expressed idea is bound to have some impact on the motivation of students, and particularly on the motivation of those who are in FE by default, rather than by choice.

There is another significant factor, too, which arises from the fact that the FE curriculum is a predominantly vocational one. This one is largely historical, and it has to do with status. Despite efforts to establish 'parity of esteem', a vocational curriculum is still widely viewed as somehow inferior to an academic one. This is a view which will inevitably have an impact on the vocational student or trainee's self-esteem. But how did this view come about?

In England two centuries ago, education usually meant a grounding in the classics. It was the grammar of Latin and Greek that gave grammar schools their name. The purpose of education, in the eighteenth and early nineteenth centuries, was to produce the cultured gentleman. Although there was recognition that a wider understanding of science was essential to the country's industrial progress, this was considered to be suitable fare for artisans, but to count for little in terms of culture. Science was 'useful'; and 'useful' smacked of industry and labour. Even those who themselves rose in fortune through industry and commerce aspired to become accepted as part of the gentry by distancing themselves from the origins of their wealth. Part of this aspiration would include a classical education for their sons (Weiner, 1981). Interestingly, a classical education was regarded as broad, in contrast with a scientific or vocational education, which was perceived to be narrow in purpose and outcome. These nineteenth-century concepts of broad and narrow are in direct contrast with their current usage in educational discourse, where the academic route is now increasingly described as narrow, and the vocational route as a broadening of the curriculum. Indeed, one of the arguments for the introduction of *Curriculum 2000* was that it would help to broaden the narrow post-16 academic curriculum. Another word used to describe the classical education was 'liberal'. We can take this to mean roughly the same as 'broad'. And it is intriguing to note that this concept of a liberal education was still operating in FE until relatively recently. In the 1970s most FE colleges would have a Liberal Studies Department whose purpose was precisely to provide a broadening or cultural element to otherwise vocational courses. Tom Sharpe presents a satirical – though some would say horribly accurate – account of such teaching in his novel *Wilt*.

While a liberal, classical education was associated with high social standing and access to positions of power, vocational education became identified with more lowly social aspirations and low-status occupations. At the same time, it was still possible to speak of a vocation in positive terms – and still is. The word 'vocation' retains its associations with such careers as the priesthood and medicine; the word 'vocational' does not.

The Taunton Report of 1868 on Education gives us a clear picture of how educational needs were being ranked according to social class. The report describes three categories of parents. The first are those who wish their children to be educated up to and beyond the age of eighteen. These parents desire classics to remain at the centre of the curriculum, because:

> *they would not wish to have what might be more readily converted into money if in any degree it tends to let their children sink in the social scale.*
>
> Maclure (1986) p. 93

In other words, such parents of high social standing would consider it beneath them to allow their children to be educated with a view to their future employment. The second category of parents are those who would wish their children to be educated to the age of sixteen, would approve of Latin if not Greek, but would also desire 'a thorough knowledge of those subjects which can be turned to practical use in business'. (Maclure, 1986, p. 94). This would include little that we would now term vocational, however. It might include English, maths, natural science and perhaps a modern language. Today we'd perhaps call these Key Skills. The third category of parents, whose children might be educated to the age of fourteen, belong to 'a class distinctly lower in the social scale' (Maclure, 1986, p. 95). They would require no classics for their children, but only reading, writing and arithmetic.

Where educational provision, as it was less than a century and a half ago, is so closely and uncritically linked in the national perception to social class and status, value judgements about the type of education to be most aspired to become inevitable. What we see in the Taunton Report is the way in which subjects acquire more status the further removed they are from the world of work; and at the same time prestige is attached to, and conclusions about social status drawn from, a lengthy education in school. Certainly these ideas are still integral to commonsense assumptions about education today, and will do nothing to build the self-esteem of many students in FE.

At the same time that the Taunton Commission were producing their report, rapid industrial expansion demanded that provision be made for industrial workers to have some form of relevant training. These were artisans, most of whom would fall somewhere in the social scale well below the Taunton Report's category-three parents. This further exacerbated the rigid linking of education and class. A technical education was, from its very origins, associated with the labouring classes. The Mechanics Institutes which were set up in the second quarter of the nineteenth century – and which we may take as the forerunners of our modern FE colleges – had a curriculum which reflected the vocational needs of employers as well as catering for workers' aspirations to learning and self-improvement. This instigated a debate over what constituted 'useful knowledge'. This was also a debate about the purposes of education and about what it meant to be educated. It is a debate which we, as professionals, have an on-going commitment to engage in.

As teachers in FE, it is important that we have a grasp of this historical background, because it explains a great deal about the way the sector is perceived today. It is a background of which it might be useful for students, too, to have an understanding. A realisation that some people's views of the sector rest on such outmoded ideas of what constitutes a 'valuable' education may help students (and teachers, too) to take a more positive view of the education or training route they find themselves upon; and as a consequence of this, they may also put a higher value on themselves and their achievements.

Linking motivation and behaviour

We've been discussing historical and social issues here; but as teachers we find ourselves dealing not with these huge driving forces, but with their consequences for the individual learner. And it's at the level of the individual that we have to develop our strategies to encourage and support student learning. The practical purpose of investigating some of the reasons why a lack of enthusiasm seems to be endemic among certain groups of our students is primarily to draw some conclusions about what teachers can and cannot expect to do about it. The argument so far in this chapter could be accused of making two broad assumptions. One is that bad or challenging behaviour can always be attributed to lack of motivation; and the other is that both can always be attributed to historical or social factors. In fact, it would be foolish to assume that both of these are always the case. People's behaviour – good or bad – is unlikely to be entirely socially conditioned. As Midgley (2001) points out, this would be like thinking of bad behaviour

> *as a set of peculiar behaviour-patterns belonging only to people with a distinctive history, people wearing, as it were, black hats like those which identify the villains in cowboy films.* (p. 4)

The reality is far more complicated than this. Not all students respond to the circumstances of their post-16 education and training by adopting a negative attitude or by losing all enthusiasm. And there is no doubt that students, like the rest of us, must take responsibility for their own behaviour.

There are other useful theories, of course, besides the social and historical ones, as to why individuals behave in ways which we might describe as 'uncooperative' or 'bad' or 'aggressive'. Such theories apply generally, and are not specific to FE students as some of the socio-historical ones are. They are, nevertheless, useful for us as teachers to bear in mind; and you will find them informing many of the ideas and suggestions in the chapters which follow. They include, for example, the theory that earlier experiences may set a pattern for our future behaviour; and that lack of self-worth may be directed outwards as anger against others (Freud). And that the feeling of being unvalued, or a fear of mockery, will both act as barriers to cooperation and learning (Rogers, Maslow). Or that hurt inflicted previously during our education may make us fearful of all teachers (Behaviourists). Or that post-modernism and the loss of absolute values has encouraged the belief that good and bad are merely relative and that there is no particular merit in being good (Rorty, 1989). And on a more mundane level there are the populist theories which blame bad behaviour on too much television or too little discipline in schools.

The teacher's role

The root causes of challenging behaviour, then, whether they be social, philosophical or psychological, are not simple pedagogical issues susceptible to being tackled on a classroom by classroom basis. So what *can* the teacher do? Well, to begin with, by acknowledging what they can't change, they will be clearer about what they can. Where the promise of an extrinsic reward (for example a job on successful completion of a course) would be viewed with cynicism by the students, the teacher can try to develop in the students an intrinsic motivation – an enjoyment of, and satisfaction in, what they are doing for its own sake. Where the student's past experiences have disinclined them to cooperate now with teachers, we can offer them a more positive model of the teacher–student relationship. Or where the student can gain little self-esteem from the nature of the course they are pursuing, the teacher can find other, positive ways to help the student to feel good about themselves, both as a learner and as a member of a group.

The 41 trainee FE teachers mentioned at the beginning of this chapter recorded in their reflective journals the experience of their first encounters with students who were unmotivated and uncooperative. At first they expressed shock and dismay at finding that there are so many students who behave in this way. For example, one writes:

> *I observed three different classes today, taught by three different teachers. None of the students seem to be able to listen to anything for more than about two minutes. Hardly anyone arrives on time. They all start asking to leave on some pretext or the other well before the end. They don't stay in their seats. They shout across the classroom. And they moan at the teacher all the time. In one class one girl kept triggering the ring tone of her phone – a sort of jingle version of the Dam Busters. The teacher pointed out that it was stopping other students from working. He asked her if she'd do that when her family was trying to watch TV. She said, really belligerently, 'Yeah? So?'*

But as they begin to see that this sort of behaviour is happening in a wide range of classes and is being experienced by a wide range of teachers, they begin to explore the idea that it cannot necessarily be laid at the door of bad teaching, nor blamed on a particular 'type' of student. They begin, in fact, to articulate explanations that do not depend on deficit models of the teacher or the student, but which draw on the sort of social, political and economic structures which we have been exploring in this chapter.

> *I'm beginning to wonder if it's overly optimistic to expect enthusiasm from students. What's in it for them, after all? Just being here at all for some of them means that they're second best. And what are they going to get out of it? A job? I doubt it – certainly not immediately. An interesting course of study? I suppose it could be. But it's so geared to work – it must just rub it in all the time that most of their chances of getting decent work in this vocational area are pretty minimal.*

The trainee lecturers' journals highlighted another issue, too. We could refer to this as the retention problem. One of them expressed it like this:

The tutors I observed today tended largely to ignore the background talking that went on in their classes. Some control was attempted, but it wasn't really sustained. One of the tutors said afterwards, when I asked her, that she doesn't feel there's much she can do about it. If she was more heavy handed, things would get confrontational. And also she's got to avoid students dropping out, because this would mean a loss of on programme funding, and it wouldn't please the college management. So she's just got to tolerate the bad manners. But surely this behaviour must get in the way of the students learning anything. So what are they here for?

Because student numbers have units of funding attached – however current policy happens to calculate it – the exclusion or expulsion of students from courses and programmes of learning carries a financial cost to the college. Inevitably this may lead to situations where unacceptable behaviour is tolerated and carries no dire consequences for the student concerned. In other words, there may, in extreme cases, be no particular expectation of students learning.

Other accounts of what is happening in FE

Of course, the snapshots we get of what is happening in FE classrooms and workshops from these teachers' journals cannot tell us the whole story. Some of the current literature on FE presents the situation quite differently. It has been argued, for example, that linking colleges' funding not only to student retention but also to student achievement will result not so much in the retention of disruptive or disengaged students as our journal-keepers suggest, but rather in a drive by colleges to only recruit more able students (Brean and Purcell, 2000). And not all researchers report a sense of disenchantment or a lack of motivation on the part of FE students (for example Ainley and Bailey, 1997). There is also evidence from some researchers that the vocational curriculum, at least in the form of the old GNVQs, actually encourages and enhances student achievement and motivation (Harkin and Davis, 1996) rather than discourages it as others have suggested. There are details of where to find these accounts, and others, in the reference section at the end of this chapter. It is interesting and worthwhile from a professional point of view to read such accounts and to weigh them against your own experience. This is one of the purposes for which a reflective journal is useful. Our continuing professional development as teachers depends not only on our ability to reflect upon our own practice and experience, but also to compare this with the research and theorising of others; to consider how our own developing theory about our role, purpose and practices compares to the wider picture and the currently accepted view of what is happening in the sector.

Conclusion

One trainee teacher wrote in her journal:

Some lecturers don't seem to expect anything of their students at all. One lecturer said to me, just be pleased if they turn up. You'll never get any work out of them.

There's not much point trying. You just have to turn up and try to stop them running riot. We're just baby sitters, really. That's what he said. But that can't be right.

She is absolutely correct, isn't she? That can't be right. As professionals, our prime responsibility is to support student learning, so avoidance of the problem by simply 'baby-sitting' difficult classes should not be an option we'd want to consider. The purpose of this book is to suggest other options and to equip the teacher with a range of strategies for motivating the unmotivated, for managing potentially challenging interactions, and for making the learning experience more comfortable and enjoyable for students and teacher alike.

References

Ainley, P. and Bailey, B. (1997) *The Business of Learning: Staff and Student Experiences of FE in the 1990s*. London: Cassell

Ball, S. (1993) Education markets, choice, and social class: the market as a class strategy in the UK and the USA. *British Journal of Sociology of Education*, 4 (1), pp. 3–19

Brean, S. and Purcell, M. (2000) Get them in – but keep them in. *The Lecturer*, February 2000, p. 11

DES (1991) *Education and Training for the 21st Century*. London: HMSO

DfES (2002) *Extending Opportunities, Raising Standards*: (*White Paper 14–19*) London: HMSO (or www.dfes.gov.uk)

Finn, D. (1987) *Training Without Jobs*. Basingstoke: Macmillan

Harkin, J. and Davis, P. (1996) The impact of GNVQs on the communication styles of teachers. *Research in Post-compulsory Education*, 1, pp. 97-107

Maclure, J. S. (ed.) (1996) *Educational Documents: England and Wales 1816 to the Present Day*. London: Methuen

Midgley, M. (2001) *Wickedness*. London: Routledge Classics

Reeves, F. (1995) *The Modernity of Further Education*. Bilston and Ticknall: Bilston College Publications and *Education Now*

Rorty, R. (1989) *Contingency, Irony and Solidarity*. Cambridge: Cambridge University Press

Wallace, S. (2002) No good surprises: intending lecturers' preconceptions and initial experiences of further education. *British Educational Research Journal*, 28 (1), pp. 79–93

Weiner, M. (1981) *English Culture and the Decline of Industrial Spirit*. Cambridge: Cambridge University Press

3 STUDENTS TALKING

It is the province of knowledge to speak and it is the privilege of wisdom to listen.
O.W. Holmes, 1872

This chapter looks at what students themselves have to say about why they are in Further Education, and what motivates them to remain there. They speak about their previous experiences of education and training and how these have shaped their attitudes. The reader is encouraged to analyse and reflect upon these accounts, and to identify ways in which what these students say may be used to inform their own planning and teaching.

The material in this chapter may be used for developing and reinforcing the following areas of skills and knowledge as set out in the FENTO Standards:

➔ b2; b3; c1; d1; d3; d5; e4; g1; g2; g3; h1; h2

It also addresses the personal attributes which FENTO lists as necessary to the FE teacher.

Personal experiences

This chapter is based on the accounts which real students have given of their experiences and perceptions of FE, and how they came to be there. In Chapter 1 we looked at a number of possible explanations of why so many students currently in FE seem to be unco-operative or poorly motivated. This sort of theorising always has its place, not least because it is useful for giving us an overview and for gaining some perspective on how our own role as teachers fits into this equation. Taken on its own, though, it will always seem a little distant from the practicalities of our day-to-day teaching until we have looked at it in terms of specific student experience. That is why we need to listen, before we go any further, to what students themselves have to say. We can't really know what being an FE student feels like until we hear the students' own accounts of their experience. As later chapters will go on to argue, we can understand best how to motivate others and encourage co-operation if we are able to imagine ourselves for a moment in their shoes.

There is surprisingly little literature, academic or otherwise, which presents FE from the student's point of view. Two notable exceptions are Ainley and Bailey (1998), who devote a section of their book to students' experience of FE; and Ball, *et al* (2000) who present detailed case studies of young people's post-16 experiences. Ainley and Bailey's sample of students seem on the whole to be reasonably well-motivated, and amenable towards the idea of continuing their education and training. Ball *et al* provide an insight into the social and economic factors which shape the choices made at 16, and argue that, in effect, these aren't really 'choices' at all. You may find that either or both of these provide a useful background to the arguments of the previous chapter and to the student accounts which are presented here.

This chapter, then, is based on what 50 FE students had to say about their experience of being in a college of FE and what led them there. The students themselves are drawn from a wide range of age-groups and backgrounds, and from every level of programme from Basic Skills Training to HNCs. The examples presented here of what they have to say are chosen as both representative and illustrative of the main issues which emerged from the accounts as a whole. The students' names and some background details have, of course, been fictionalised in order to maintain their anonymity.

Lester and Kylie

Task

Read through the case study below. What general points would you want to make about this student's motivation and trajectory?

Lester

Lester is in his first year of FE and is studying three A levels: Sociology, History and Law. His ambition is to go on to Higher Education and get a Law degree which he'll then use to train as a solicitor. Here's what he says:

Lester: *I didn't do that well at school. Nobody expected me to do that well. And I didn't. They wouldn't let me stay to take A levels at school. They thought I was a waste of time.*

Interviewer: *Why do you think that was?*

Lester: *Because of my ethnic group. They just think, oh well, he'll end up driving a taxi or something. Being on the dole or something. So they couldn't be bothered. That's what I think, anyway. But it's different here* [FE College]. *They treat you different. There's more respect. It's like you're independent. It's like you're an adult. And the teachers are all more relaxed. They talk to you like you're all people – not teacher and students but just all people, all working together.*

Interviewer: *And what about the subjects you're studying? Do you enjoy those?*

Lester: *I do enjoy them, yes. Because I chose them. My dad wanted me to be an engineer. He wanted me to do all sciences. All my family had this thing about me being an engineer. But that wasn't what I wanted to do. I chose what I wanted to do because I knew I'd enjoy it. And I know where I want to go with it, and I'm going to get there. Because it's my life, do you know what I mean?*

Discussion

The first thing that's likely to strike you about this, I think, is that Lester is a perfect illustration of what we all know FE should be about. In a way he represents the ideal – the sort of student that teachers entering the FE sector expect to find. Traditionally FE has always been viewed by those who work within it as the sector of the second chance. Students who did not flourish at school; students whom – it might be said – were failed by their schooling; these were the students for whom FE provided a second opportunity to discover their potential. And the success of FE in this respect was always partly attributed to its less formal atmosphere, its more relaxed styles of teacher–student interaction, and the scope it provided for students to make their own choices. Lester conforms to this model exactly. Whatever the truth of his assertions about the assumptions made at his school, there is no doubt that he feels he has gained more validation and respect in FE.

His account reassures us that FE can still work like this. The question we have to ask ourselves is, why do more students not feel as Lester does? Part of the answer, of course, may lie in what he has to say about choice.

> *I do enjoy them, yes. Because I chose them … I chose what I wanted to do because I knew I'd enjoy it.*

As we saw in Chapter One, for many students their presence in FE does not reflect choice, and nor does it present them with any choices once there. There is also the question of trajectory: having a clear, attainable target in mind clearly plays an important part in Lester's motivation.

> *And I know where I want to go with it, and I'm going to get there. Because it's my life, do you know what I mean?*

Choice and a worthwhile trajectory may be luxuries which not all students believe are available to them.

Task

Have a look now at a student who is the same age as Lester but whose account of FE reads very differently. As you read through it, make a note of those factors which seem to have contributed to the different perception of the sector.

Kylie

Kylie also did not do particularly well at school. None of her GCSEs were above grade E. She has come to college to retake four of these.

Kylie: *Why did I come to this college? This particular one? It's near my house, isn't it. Why a college? Because I had to retake my GCSEs. If I haven't got them I can't do anything, can I?*

Interviewer: *How are you enjoying it?*

Kylie: *Childcare's alright. It's easy. I quite like that. That's my best one. I hate Sociology. It's rubbish. The teacher's stupid. You can't even talk to her. She's just like, 'Shut up and get on with it.' And I'm like, 'If that's the way you feel about it— 'You know? She can stick it. Nobody likes her. We just don't turn up. There used to be about 20 of us. Hardly anybody goes now. What's the point of it, anyway? Even if I got it, what am I going to do? I'll never get my maths. You can't get a job without maths. Not a proper job anyway.*

Discussion

Something that's immediately apparent here is the narrowness of the parameters within which Kylie feels she can make her choices. The way she sees it, she *had* to retake GCSEs to stand any chance of further progression. To do this she *had* to go to an FE college. Now that she's there she *has* to do maths because, 'You can't get a job without maths. Not a proper job anyway.' But she doesn't feel she has much hope of getting her maths, so the question that must be springing to her mind all the time is, *Why is she there at all?* She's there to get the GCSEs that will allow her to progress; but she isn't (according to her) going to get them. And so we have a perfect recipe here for demotivation and disengagement. From where we stand we know she could have chosen an alternative Intermediate programme. We can see that she should have been offered more constructive careers advice somewhere along the line. But our knowing that doesn't help Kylie at the point at which she currently finds herself. Her predicament illustrates for us how easily that second chance which the FE sector offers can fail to materialise.

There's another factor in her account, too, which will draw our particular attention as teachers.

> *I hate Sociology. It's rubbish. The teacher's stupid. You can't even talk to her. She's just like, 'Shut up and get on with it.'*

Sociology teachers need take no offence here! This could have been any subject at all. The general point is that students will not usually enjoy the subject if they don't like the teacher. There are a number of ways in which we might understand that word, 'like', as we shall see in the chapters which follow. It is not necessarily about warm, fuzzy feelings; it can even be something which is better expressed as a wary respect. And there are many reasons why a student might dislike a teacher. In Kylie's case the problem seems to be that she finds the teacher unapproachable and unsympathetic. What we might take from this is that it behoves us always to give due emphasis to the teacher–student relationship. When this relationship is working positively, it constitutes one of our most powerful means of raising student motivation. For Kylie – who knows? – it could have made all the difference to how she felt about herself and her future prospects.

Tony and Aaron

The next two students are older than Lester and Kylie. They fall into the category of Adult Learners. Both of them are classed as having learning difficulties. Their names are Tony and Aaron.

Task

Read through Aaron's and Tony's accounts of their FE experience and identify the factors which seem to contribute (a) to these students' motivation; and (b) to triggering inappropriate behaviour.

Aaron

Aaron is in his early twenties and was diagnosed at school as having moderate learning difficulties. He has been a student in FE for over six years. On first leaving school he attended a Basic Skills programme in order to improve his communication skills. He then enrolled on a regional Intermediate programme of Land-based Studies. From this he has progressed to an NVQ 1 in Horticulture.

Aaron: *I do it because that's what I like. My mum said, 'Go on, then. It's time we had a gardener in the family.' Because she thinks it's about gardening.*

Interviewer: *What do you like best about it?*

Aaron: *I like doing things. I like it when we have to do things and we go out and we really do it. I don't like it when we have to read stuff or just watch stuff. That's when I mess about. I don't like it when we just have to listen. I don't like writing the lists because they go too quick and I can't do that so I don't like it. I just mess about. And I don't like Mr [X] because he shouts at you and he makes you stay out when it's raining and you get soaked. I like doing computers. And I like it when it's just like a few of you – just a few of you and the teacher. Or just me and the teacher because then he helps me.*

Interviewer: *So do you enjoy college, then?*

Aaron: *It's cool, yeah. Everybody here's my friends. And so are the teachers an' all.*

Tony

Tony is in his thirties and has left the army after a head injury which has affected his speech and his short-term memory. He enrolled at the college on the recommendation of his neurologist, as part of his recovery programme. Initially he found himself placed on a Life Skills programme for students with moderate to severe learning difficulties. He didn't feel this was appropriate to his particular needs, and the frustration he felt over this resulted in some episodes of aggressive behaviour. He is now on a personalised learning support programme.

Tony: *I can't remember stuff. I have to keep learning it. I can't remember. I do it, and then they say to me, 'We did this last week.' And it scares me. Sometimes there's words and I can't – you know. There's things I'm meaning to say but it's like there isn't a word. And they're looking at me, you know? They're thinking I'm thick. But I'm not thick. It gets me – you know – I just go ballistic. It's all in here, you know?*

Interviewer: *What's your goal at the moment?*

Tony: *Get the memory back.*

Interviewer: *And is college helping you with this, do you think?*

Tony: *Well, nothing else is, is it? It's down to me in the end. It's down to me to show them I'm not stupid. If I can't do that, I might as well jack it in now.*

Discussion

One of the most useful things about Aaron's account is that he expresses so clearly what motivates him and what causes him to 'mess about'. The bottom line is that he is motivated by those activities he enjoys, and switched off by those he finds boring or too difficult. Now, this might seem so obvious as to be hardly worth saying; but it raises some interesting issues. A student might also be switched off, after all, by activities they find too easy. It's not enough, then, to say that we can best motivate students by only making demands of them that are well within their reach. What Aaron's account more accurately illustrates is the importance of making the learning experience as free as possible from anxiety. Aaron isn't motivated by tasks he fears he'll fail at. He isn't motivated by being shouted at, and he has no enthusiasm for lessons which involve physical discomfort. He also has a preferred style of learning, which is to be actively engaged rather than be a passive recipient. When he is actively engaged he does not 'mess about.' Given the numbers of students we teach, we don't always make the connection between student behaviour and a particular style of learning activity. However, this will almost always repay careful attention when it comes to planning and evaluating lessons.

We see the concept of choice raised here, too. Aaron is quite clear about the fact that the subject and occupation he is pursuing is one which he has chosen himself because it's something he enjoys. This sense of having made a genuine choice is something that he shares with Lester; and it is probably no coincidence that both these students declare themselves to be well-motivated and happy with the FE experience. There's one more factor, too, that Aaron's very clear about, and that is that being in FE involves being among friends. In counting the teachers (as well as fellow students) as friends, Aaron provides another illustration of the important role that the teacher–learner relationship plays in student motivation.

Tony's account raises rather different, but equally important issues. In his case the issue of motivation is perhaps a little more complicated. Attendance at FE is tied up with his determination to recover. In this respect he seems to be experiencing very little sense of choice here. FE is for him not so much a second chance as an only chance – in his case, of recovering his old self. Indeed, his account is a reminder to us, if we need one, of how important the student's sense of self is as a factor affecting their behaviour and motivation. Tony feels he has been put in the wrong category; that his innate ability and his previous achievements have somehow been discounted and devalued. Frustration at this has made him behave badly and it has also, in undermining his self-esteem, served to discourage and demotivate him. There is a lesson for us here about the need to acknowledge students' existing abilities and achievements, whatever they may be. If we fail to do this we will find we are operating exclusively within the deficiency model of the student. That is, we will see only what the student is still lacking in terms of knowledge, attitude and skills. We won't see the whole student, and we will miss the opportunity to build on their sense of self-worth, which is vital to effective learning.

Rina and Sara

The next two students we'll hear from are both adult returners who have enrolled on demanding courses despite their earlier negative experiences of education. Rina is on an Access to HE course. Sara is studying for an HNC in Fashion and Design. As you read through what they have to say below, note down any general issues as well as any which you believe are particularly important to our understanding of adult returners' needs and expectations.

Rina

I did really badly at school, me. I didn't even get put in for some of the GCSEs. They thought it was a waste of time. They didn't like me very much, I don't think, the teachers. They couldn't be bothered with me. When I did something stupid they used to get the other kids laughing at me. So I suppose I knew I was rubbish, really. And when I finished at sixteen I had a few jobs working in shops and that, and then I got married. I was only eighteen when I got married, and I had a family and that. Two kids. And I kept thinking, I ought to go back and do something. But I daren't, you know? I didn't want that whole thing of feeling like I was no good at it – like I was thick. And also I felt like really I should be looking after the kiddies. Or I should at least be earning something so I can buy them stuff. I still feel like that, really. I still feel guilty about the kids. It took me ten years to come back, and I was terrified. Even now I don't really believe I'm going to get anywhere. I still have days when I think the teachers don't like me. I'm sure they think – you know – 'Oh it's her. She's just thick.' Or they laugh about me. Laugh about me wanting to go to university. Like, 'In your dreams.'

Sara

I was a right tearaway at school. I was, honest! I used to get teased when I was little because I was so good and I was a bit of a boff. But once you started playing the teachers up – that was how you made friends. You were either in with the teachers and you had no friends, or you gave the teachers a hard time and then you were really popular. That's how it was at our school. And in the end I was a natural at it. I wouldn't let anybody tell me what to do. I was horrible! I bet they were right pleased when I left. I was only sixteen, but I started working in a bar. I worked in a few bars, but I never really did a proper job. I was messing about like that for nearly eight years. And then I started going out with Rich and he said why didn't I go and do some proper qualifications and get a proper job. And I thought, yeah, I can do that. But I was that scared. It was like if I went back they'd start trying to boss me about again. They'd start trying to tell me what to do. And also there was the money. I've still got a bar job in the evenings – unbelievable! And sometimes I'm rushing round, you know, and I don't get my college work done properly because I've got to get to work. Or I'm working late and I get into College all tired and ratty and I start giving the teachers a hard time. It's easy to slip back into it, that's the trouble. When you've been like that you see a teacher and it sort of sets you off. Even though you know they're really nice people. It's funny, that.

Discussion

What Rina and Sara illustrate all too well is the fact that FE students come to us carrying all the baggage of their previous educational experience. In the case of adult returners, that can be very heavy baggage indeed. The implications for us, as teachers, can be quite daunting. Both Rina and Sara have a very negative memory of teachers – Rina because she believes hers thought her stupid (and whether the picture she paints of them is accurate or not, the important point is how she now feels about it).

> *They didn't like me very much, I don't think, the teachers. They couldn't be bothered with me. When I did something stupid they used to get the other kids laughing at me.*

And Sara because they represented an authority she had decided to rebel against.

> *It was like if I went back they'd start trying to boss me about again. They'd start trying to tell me what to do.*

What happens, then, when students like Rina and Sara come into FE, is that they bring this impression of teachers with them, and it becomes our task to establish a more constructive model for them of what a teacher does and is. The aggression and resistance we can sometimes encounter from students may in reality be directed at some teacher or teachers who upset them or left them feeling negative about themselves a long time ago. This is important for us to bear in mind if we are not to turn such encounters into trench warfare.

In terms of issues which are pertinent to adult returners in particular, what we are reminded of here in Rina's and Sara's accounts is that the lives of adult returners to FE are complicated. As well as all the other baggage, they often have family responsibilities, conflicting priorities, financial commitments, a sense of guilt at taking time away from the children, their partners, their domestic responsibilities. This can affect their motivation and mood, as well as their capacity to give their full attention to their college work.

> *And sometimes I'm rushing round, you know, and I don't get my college work done properly because I've got to get to work. Or I'm working late and I get into College all tired and ratty and I start giving the teachers a hard time.*

In other words, the adult student we see in our class may be only the tip of the iceberg. There may be a multiplicity of roles and responsibilities which we never see, but which will impact upon the way the student relates to us and to their learning.

Lee, Abdul, Deb, Gaz, Richie, Jo, Brendan

For our remaining examples, let's go back to some sixteen- and seventeen-year-old students. When we talk about motivation and behaviour in FE this is usually the age group we have in mind as presenting us with the greatest challenge. We'll have a look, therefore, at what some of them have to say about us, their teachers. Some of this may make for uncomfortable reading – but it's nothing we can't handle!

Task

As you go through this section, you should consider:

- ***What can we learn from these students' accounts about the qualities in a teacher they seem to respond well to?***
- ***What behaviours or qualities in their teachers seem to have the effect of discouraging, demotivating or antagonising them?***

Lee

[Teacher X], *she's great. She's a good laugh. She makes it funny. And you can tell she's enjoying herself. Teachers always give up with me, but she just won't give up. And you can't, like, rattle her cage. She never shouts or nothing. She has this look, you know. This look – and then the next minute she's laughing again. So I turn up for her lessons. They're alright.*

Abdul

It's like he can't be bothered. He doesn't want to be there. You can tell he doesn't want to be there. Well that's alright, innit? Because we don't want to be there either.

Deb

I was really surprised when he said, 'Call me [X].' I didn't think you call teachers by their first name. You never call teachers by their first name at school. But it's like he wants to be a person, like you're two people and feel like you can talk to him. And if you don't do the work or something, he doesn't get mad, he gets worried about you. And he says, 'Is everything alright?' and stuff like that. So you know he's really bothered. So you don't get scared about handing stuff in to him because you know he's not going to get mad with you if it's rubbish.

Gaz

He's just pathetic. He never looks at you. We just do what we want. Half the time he looks like he's scared, and half the time he shouts. Completely loses it. It's well funny. His face goes all red and that. Nobody takes any notice of what he says. He hates us and we don't give a — about him.

Richie

She really knows what she's talking about. That's the thing about her. And she likes it, you know? And that makes you like it as well. Because it's interesting. And she listens to you. Like, when you answer a question or something, she listens to you like she's really interested. And if you get it wrong or something, it doesn't matter, you know? She's like, 'Well that's an interesting way of looking at it, Richie.' And she's like, 'Good try.' And all like that. You feel like she's really pleased with you, know what I mean? That's why I go.

Jo

Even the teachers think it's boring. Like there's this one teacher and she says, 'Right, we've got to do this thing this morning and I know it's boring and that, but we've got to do it.' And you think, well, if even the teacher thinks it's boring, what's the point? I'd rather be having a laugh and that.

Brendan

He makes you work. He doesn't shout or nothing. He just looks at you. You can have a laugh with him though. He never disrespects you or nothing. And we don't disrespect him. His lessons are alright.

Discussion

So, first of all, what behaviours or qualities in their teachers seem to have the effect of discouraging, demotivating or antagonising these students? Perhaps we could summarise them thus:

- Lack of enthusiasm: 'It's like he can't be bothered.'
- Lack of commitment: 'He doesn't want to be there.'
- Shows no interest in the students: 'You can tell he doesn't want to be there.'
- Lack of self-confidence: 'Half the time he looks like he's scared.'
- Lack of assertiveness: 'We just do what we want.'
- Loss of temper: 'Half the time he shouts. Completely loses it.'
- Hostility: 'He hates us.'
- No interest in the subject: 'I know it's boring and that, but we've got to do it.'

This makes rather dismal reading. We can reassure ourselves with the knowledge that there are very few teachers who conform to this model. They simply wouldn't survive, for one thing. But there's one important purpose this list serves, and that is to confirm that what we do as teachers does make a difference. However heavily social and economic factors may impact on students' behaviour and motivation, what we do and the way we relate towards our students can have considerable impact too.

Now, on a more positive note, what can we learn from these students' accounts about the qualities in a teacher they seem to respond well to?

The list you came up with here probably looked something like this.

- Sense of humour: 'She's a good laugh. She makes it funny.'
- Enthusiasm: 'And you can tell she's enjoying herself.'
- Commitment: 'She just won't give up.'

- Assertiveness: 'She has this look, you know.'
- Openness and approachability: 'But it's like he wants to be a person, like you're two people and feel like you can talk to him.'
- Care and empathy: 'He doesn't get mad, he gets worried about you.'
- Sound knowledge of the subject: 'She really knows what she's talking about.'
- Acceptance and encouragement: 'She listens to you like she's really interested.'
- Personal impact: 'He makes you work. He doesn't shout or nothing. He just looks at you.'
- Respect for learners: 'He never disrespects you or nothing. And we don't disrespect him. His lessons are alright.'

These, then, are the qualities or attributes in the teacher which are, according to these accounts, most likely to motivate students and encourage manageable behaviour. It's interesting at this point to compare them to the list drawn up by FENTO (2001) of the 'personal attributes teachers and teaching teams should possess and display'. These are:

- personal impact and presence;
- enthusiasm;
- self-confidence;
- energy and persistence;
- reliability;
- intellectual rigour;
- integrity;
- appreciation of FE values and ethics;
- commitment to education and to learners' progress and achievement;
- realism;
- openness and responsiveness to others;
- acceptance of differing learning needs, expectations and styles;
- empathy, rapport and respect for learners and colleagues;
- assertiveness.

You can find these on the FENTO website at www.fento.org.

Taken as a list, these look like a tall order; and it may be that none of us can quite live up to all of the list all of the time. Perhaps that's why FENTO adds that phrase, '... and teaching teams'. If one of your colleagues is suffering from flagging energy on a particular day, for example, you can step in with the energy for two! What is certainly apparent, however, is that this list makes sense; not only because it corresponds with what the students themselves are telling us, but also because we can recognise it from our own experience of teaching and being taught. Elsewhere I have written about the 'Best Teacher' (Wallace, 2001). The qualities and attributes we have just been considering are the ones most often cited when people are asked to define 'best teacher' in terms of their own experience of learning. In the chapters that follow we shall see some examples of what happens when this model of teaching is applied to motivating students and managing their behaviour; and we shall also see some examples of what happens when it is not.

References

Ainley, P. and Bailey, B. (1997) *The Business of Learning: Staff and Student Experiences of FE in the 1990s*. London: Cassell

Ball, S., Maguire, M. and Macrae, S. (2000) *Choice, Pathways and Transitions Post-16*. London: Routledge-Falmer

Wallace, S. (2001) *Teaching and Supporting Learning in Further Education: Meeting the FENTO Standards*. Exeter: Learning Matters

Websites

FENTO – www.fento.org

4 WHERE DO WE START?

'Begin at the beginning,' the King said, gravely,
'and go on till you come to the end: then stop.'
Lewis Carroll, 1865

This chapter is about identifying the importance of the student's starting point, and using it. It suggests ways in which the teacher can find and build on what is positive, and also on what simply *is*. In the process, it examines how students may be motivated by challenging and modifying their construct of 'the teacher'.

The material in this chapter may be used for developing and reinforcing the following areas of skills and knowledge as set out in the FENTO Standards:

➔ a1; a2; d1; d3; d4; e1; e2; e3; e4; g1; g2; g3; h1; h2

It also provides an opportunity to consider the personal attributes of the FE teacher which are listed by FENTO.

Communication

We began the practical chapters of this book by looking at what students have to say about their learning. There is good reason why this was the appropriate place to begin. Our starting point – if we want to motivate and engage our students – should always be the learner, whether we are planning our teaching or reflecting on our practice. Understanding the needs and attitudes which the learner brings to the classroom or the workshop is an essential first step in establishing a positive learning environment. It is, it could be argued, more important in the first instance than translating the syllabus or course specifications into a scheme of work. If the scheme of work you've designed is incompatible with your students' need for constant reassurance or active learning or note-taking skills, for example, it's unlikely to be particularly effective in achieving the required learning outcomes.

Hearing what students have to say, however, is not always straightforward. In the previous chapter we heard from students who were willing and able to express their views and their feelings about what motivated them and what didn't; and how their previous experiences of learning had affected their current needs. When students are able to do this, and we are able to listen and hear, we have a useful basis on which to build, both in terms of our professional relationship with them, and the way in which we structure their learning. However, not all our students will communicate such information to us so easily; or they may communicate it in ways which are not immediately evident; ways which may seem more like a challenge than an attempt at communication.

Andy

Let's have a look at one of Andy's classes. Andy is working towards a PGCE in FE (a FENTO Stage 3 equivalent). As part of his course requirement his teaching of this class is being video-taped, so that he can review it and write a self-evaluation. His tutor is also present, sitting at the back of the class, to write a formal report on his teaching. It is a GCSE English Language class. There are twelve students, six male and six female, all aged between 16 and 19. This is only the third lesson he has had with them. Here is what the video camera sees:

> The tables are arranged in a horseshoe, and Andy starts by sitting on the teacher's table at the front of the class and briefing the students on the task they're about to do. They'll each be given a picture on which to base a piece of descriptive writing. There is silence as he speaks. Most of the students appear to be listening. One or two are making notes.
>
> Andy then gives out the pictures, one to each student, as he walks around the inside of the horseshoe of tables. As he does so, he checks with each of them that they understand the task and that they have paper and pens with them. The students are cooperative, even enthusiastic – nodding, asking questions, picking up their pictures and looking at them with interest. Then he comes to a young woman – Nicola – who responds very differently. She doesn't look at him. She doesn't respond to him. When he sets a picture down for her on her desk she simply folds her arms on the table in front of her and lowers her head down on to them as though she was going to sleep. Andy hovers there for a moment or two, looking uncertain; but then moves on to the last two students, who respond positively like the others. He goes back to the front of the class, asks whether there are any questions and, receiving no response, tells them to begin the task, for which they have twenty minutes.
>
> As the students work, he moves around the room, inside the horseshoe, giving help and asking questions. The first time he approaches Nicola's table she sees him coming and starts packing her things away, putting her pencil case and folder back into her bag and pushing the picture away from her to the far side of the desk. Then she puts her head down on her arms again. Andy hunkers down so that he's not looming over her, and says, 'Come on, Nicola. Let's see what you've written.'
>
> No movement. No response.
>
> 'Come on. What's the matter? Don't you like the picture?'
>
> No response
>
> 'Do you want another picture?'
>
> Still no response.
>
> Andy waits a moment, stands up, glances towards his tutor, and then moves off to help other students.

The second time Andy approaches her table, Nicola, still head down, begins slowly tapping her forehead against her table – not hard, but audibly, nevertheless. She hasn't looked at her picture. Her pens and folder are still in her bag. Andy hunkers down again. He says: 'Come on, Nicola. What are you doing?'

No response.

'Come on. Don't do that. You'll hurt yourself.'

No response. Andy looks uncertainly towards his tutor. Then he says:

'Come on, Nicola. Let's have a look at that picture. Let's see what we want to say about it.'

No response.

Andy remains there a moment or two, then stands up and moves on to the next student, who is working well and who, like the others, responds to him in a friendly way.

When the twenty minutes for the task are almost up and Andy has almost completed his third circuit of the room, he approaches Nicola again. This time, as she sees him coming, she begins banging her forehead more forcibly against her desk. Bang. Bang. Bang. Andy stops in his tracks and, raising his voice above the murmur of on-task noise, he says: 'OK. Time's up. You've all worked very hard. Let's take a ten minute break. Back in here at quarter past.'

The students, who hadn't been expecting a break, file out happily, chatting. Nicola goes with them, leaving behind her bag and her coat just like the rest of them. Andy looks over towards his tutor, frowning. And the camera switches off.

Task

Take some time to read this account through again, and consider the following questions:

- ***How would you feel if you were the teacher and this was happening to you?***
- ***What would you have done in these circumstances?***
- ***Do you notice anything on the second reading that you missed on the first – anything that might help you to interpret what was happening here?***

Discussion

It's important to reflect about how you would feel in this situation, because the way we feel affects the sort of decisions we make. What's happening here is an example of student behaviour which seems to be escalating out of control. It begins as non-engagement or non-cooperation, but quickly becomes something more than that. If it were simply 'bad' behaviour, such as shouting, swearing, refusing to settle down, we would at least have models in mind of how to deal with it – even if they weren't very effective models. The problem here is that we're being challenged by behaviour for which we don't have a ready-made strategy. This is likely to leave us feeling some degree of apprehension, or even panic. And of course, when we're in the grip of such a feeling, we're less likely to think clearly, and less likely to make sound decisions. This is why classroom situations such as the one Andy finds himself in are so challenging for the teacher. It's obvious that a decision has to be made, that some action has to be quickly taken. But what's the right one?

So, would you have called a break at this juncture? It's a tricky question, particularly if a mid-session break is in contravention of college rules. As you reflect on what you would have done, you may like to discuss your ideas with a colleague or mentor, or record your thinking in your reflective journal.

A couple of points which become more evident on second reading are, firstly, that Nicola was 'acting up'. That is, she was aiming her behaviour at Andy, making sure that he was approaching and could see clearly what she was doing before beginning to bang her forehead on the table, for example. Secondly, she seems to intend coming back into the class after the break. Both of these points are likely to have bearing on how we begin to interpret her behaviour.

Let's look now at what Andy has to say about how this situation made him feel, and how he initially interprets Nicola's behaviour.

Reflective journal

October 14th

Well, I wasn't looking forward to that lesson, with a camera there and my tutor. Weird thing was, what I was worried about was that the students wouldn't be able to settle because of the camera – that they'd play about or clam up. But I think because it was set up in the back corner, there was only really me who was aware of it once the lesson got going. And then I forgot about it as well because I found myself completely thrown by Nicola T's bizarre behaviour. It was like a bad dream. Here was this class, looking all interested and working well, and then suddenly there's Nicola acting more and more oddly. It just got worse. First she looked bored. Then she started banging her head on the table! And then she started banging it really hard – and I thought, '—! What's she going to do next? Pick the table up and throw it at somebody? Leap out the window?' So I called a break. I couldn't think what else to do. She just wasn't responding to anything I said.

The thing is, I found I spent the whole time, the whole lesson, focusing my thoughts on that one student. And there were 11 others, all working really hard, all deserving my attention, all deserving lots of positive feedback and praise. And I couldn't think about anything except how do I stop Nicola cracking her skull against that table. Now, that can't be right, can it? And what's worse, I don't even know what the matter was. Did she find the task too hard? Was there something about the picture I gave her that upset her? Or was it something that had gone wrong at home? Boyfriend trouble? Violence? I don't know. How am I supposed to know if she won't tell me? Complete mystery to me. At least when she came back after the break she didn't do any more head banging. Just put her head down and went to sleep. Thank goodness for small mercies.

Discussion

We can probably all empathise with what Andy was feeling here. He sums up very well the dilemma of the teacher who finds themselves in this situation.

> *I have all these learners deserving of my time and energy; and yet all my attention is taken up by this one student.*

He goes straight to the heart of things here. The teacher's prime purpose is to facilitate and support student learning. Anything which detracts from this must be addressed and resolved. What this means for us in practice is that we can't deal in the long run with situations like this simply by ignoring the difficult student. Even if her behaviour is not distracting other students from their learning, it is certainly telling us that she herself is not engaged nor on task. We see here how Andy is at a loss to interpret Nicola's behaviour; but he is absolutely right to assume that it is saying something. It is saying something about how she feels and why. It's a form of communication, albeit an oblique and very troublesome one. It is often useful to bear this in mind when confronted by challenging behaviour. We can't always hope to understand what it's saying. But it's saying something.

Let's see now how Andy's tutor unpacks and explains this in a little more detail when she writes up her observation for Andy to read.

Observation of Practical Teaching

Date:	October 14th
Subject:	English Language GCSE
Number of Students:	12

Planning and resources

Your introduction to the lesson was clear, and you briefed the students well for the task, allowing them plenty of time to ask questions and seek clarification. The task itself was appropriate – both interesting and challenging – and you'd chosen some interesting pictures to use. I like the way you moved from student to student, engaging with them one-to-one while they were working, and asking just the right questions to encourage them and move them forward.

Communication and quality of learning

It appeared to me that you get on well with these students. You seem to have established a good relationship with them, and they're prepared to work hard for you. You should give yourself credit for this. You deserve it. I say this because I imagine that what is preoccupying you at the moment is the problem with Nicola. Please don't lose sight of the fact that for most of your students this was an enjoyable and productive learning experience; and you'll see this, I'm sure, when you get around to watching the video.

Points to consider for future practice

You told me immediately after the lesson that you didn't think you'd handled the problem with Nicola very well. I think the difficulty here is that we have to have some idea what the problem might be before we can make any sensible decision about how to handle it. One thing which was clear to me, as an observer, was that Nicola was aiming these histrionics at you. She wasn't just generally expressing how she felt; she wanted to communicate this specifically to you – escalating the dramatic behaviour whenever you were looking at her. My guess is that she wanted you to ask her what was wrong. She'd probably have said, 'Nothing' – until you'd asked her a sufficient number of times; but she wouldn't have worked so hard at showing you how she felt unless she wanted this question posing somehow, in some form: 'What's wrong?'

Perhaps the answer's simply that she thought the proposed task was too easy, and wanted you to know she felt bored. But there's always the possibility, of course, that it's something far more serious than that – something which it would be more appropriate for her to discuss with a student counsellor rather than with her teacher. That's why I think you were correct not to push her for an answer in the middle of the lesson. I also think, given the alarming way her behaviour was escalating, that you were right to call a break. This was a good way to defuse things – let some steam out of the pressure cooker. It needn't have been a fully-fledged coffee break, however. Just a, 'OK. Have a couple of minutes to take a break, have a chat, stand up to stretch your legs a bit.' That sort of thing. Under cover of the chatter you might have been able to get Nicola to give you some indication of what the matter was.

As the situation stands, you know Nicola has a problem, but you don't know what it is. I think the best course would be to ask your section head if she'll have a word with her. Although Nicola is clearly targeting you and seems to want you to ask what's wrong, this could just potentially put you in a difficult or embarrassing situation as a young male teacher. Whatever her problem, she chose to remain in your class. She could easily have escaped at the break if just being there was so unbearable. She preferred to carry on performing her drama to you. That's why I think this situation needs handling with care.

Close focus

Do you think the tutor has made a fair assessment of the situation? Is there anything here you would challenge? You may like to discuss this with a colleague or mentor, or use these questions as a starting point for recording your thoughts in your reflective journal.

Discussion

We began by talking about starting points. One way of expressing this is the need to know where our students are 'coming from'. Andy's plight illustrates this perfectly; and these are some of the things we can learn from it.

- Challenging behaviour is a form of communication. It tells us the student is experiencing a problem, even if it doesn't tell us what that problem is.
- We can't begin to help a student to learn until we know where she's coming from.
- When considering a student's starting point we shouldn't be thinking of it only in terms of their current knowledge and skills, but also in terms of their level of motivation, their state of mind, and their prior experience of learning.
- The challenging behaviour of just one student can affect our ability as teachers to give sufficient support and attention to the other learners in our class.
- It is our professional responsibility, therefore, to seek some solution, although this does not necessarily mean we must solve the problem ourselves.

Understanding students' attitudes

Knowing where our students are coming from can often mean having to take into account their prior experience of learning. Teaching in FE, we are going to encounter students who, *as a minimum*, have already spent eleven years in the education system; some of them may have spent even longer. Their attitudes towards education will already have been formed. And by the very nature of FE – sometimes thought of as the sector of the second chance – many of these students' experiences of education will not have been positive ones. That is to say, they will perhaps not have experienced the pleasure of success, or have received very much praise, or have gained much self-esteem from their prior experiences of learning. Moreover, they may have formed a construct of 'the teacher' which is not a particularly positive one.

Just as every teacher and aspiring teacher will have a personal ideal – a construct of 'the perfect teacher' based on their own best experiences of being taught (Wallace, 2001), so too will every student have an idea that pops into his or her head at the sound of that word: 'teacher'. Sadly, in many cases, this idea will carry associations of oppression, of a control that's resented. It may trigger memories of being criticised or thwarted, or simply being made to do something they didn't want to do, either because it didn't interest them or it was beyond their abilities and left them open to ridicule. The student's construct of 'the teacher' is very powerful. As you stand in front of a class for the first time, happily assuming that these students are seeing you – a perfectly pleasant and caring professional whose intention is to help them learn and to enjoy themselves in the process – what some students may be seeing is something completely different. Imagine it as though a cinema projector was superimposing upon your pleasant and friendly features the threatening face, sewn together Frankenstein style, of all the teachers who, however unwittingly, have made these students feel bad about themselves and resistant to learning.

Close focus

So what can you do about it?

How can you identify whether this barrier exists?

If you find it does exist, how can you begin to deal with it so that you can be effective in supporting your students' learning?

Discussion

You'll know whether this barrier exists from your student's attitude. The clue is usually when your own positive approach and best efforts meet with rudeness, aggression, non-cooperation. As for what to do about it, the first rule is:

Don't take it personally

Admittedly, this is far more easily said than done. But it helps if you keep in mind that this is, in all probability, not about you at all, but about how this student has come to feel about 'being taught'.

As for how you begin to deal with it – well, this is an attitude that has built up in the student over several years, and so it is unlikely that you'll solve it in a moment. Given our analysis of the problem, it's clear that one answer must lie in getting the student to revise his or her notion of 'the teacher' – from someone who makes them feel bad about themselves to someone who helps them build their self-esteem and sense of achievement. This will take time; and, of course, in the face of persistently challenging behaviour, it's by no means an easy thing to do.

Why not just use strict rules and punishments? Wouldn't this be easier? We'll be looking more closely at the idea of Rules in the next chapter; and it's only commonsense that certain rules – agreed parameters of acceptable behaviour – are necessary in any environment where people are working together. However, seeking to adjust students' behaviour simply through the application of rules and punishment will always have a limited effect. It might or might not prove useful in terms of control; but it will not necessarily be effective in encouraging student learning. To become willing and effective learners, students have to feel some degree of intrinsic motivation – motivation that comes from within themselves. Students who are intrinsically motivated are more likely to engage actively with their learning, and to develop into lifelong learners. This will happen because they come to find learning, in some sense, personally rewarding. In simple terms, it makes them feel good. Extrinsic motivation, on the other hand – getting the student to learn by using threats of punishment or offers of reward – might achieve a short-term behavioural change, but leave untouched the student's basic attitude towards learning. If we are to produce a society of lifelong learners – a phrase constantly recurring in current policy statements on education – then it is students' attitudes that we need to address. If the desire to learn comes from within, then all the rest follows.

The idea of changing students' attitudes, of helping them to develop an intrinsic motivation to learn, can sound somewhat idealistic, perhaps, given some of our experiences as teachers in FE. However, as we saw in Chapter 1, the possibilities for using extrinsic motivation to encourage student learning are becoming more and more limited. We can no longer say with conviction to students on 'vocational' courses, 'Work hard and there'll be a job at the end.' We know this will not necessarily be true. We can no longer say to the student with confrontational behaviour, 'Behave, or you'll be out.' The unit of funding he carries will weigh heavily against such a step being endorsed. The reality is that such a carrot and stick approach is increasingly ineffective, even if we wanted to use it.

This brings us back, then, to helping the student to find their own motivation to learn. We've looked already at two steps we might take towards achieving this.

- Discover the student's starting point. Get to know the student.
- Help the student to revise their negative construct of Learning and The Teacher.

The next step – setting parameters of acceptable behaviour – will be achieved much more effectively if it follows on these two. It's a step which we'll look at in some detail in the next chapter. For now, we can summarise the strategy like this:

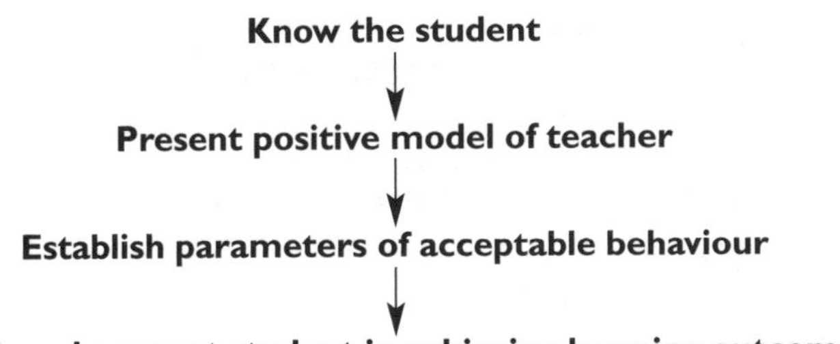

Changing the way students feel about their learning

So, how do we ensure that learning, whatever it has meant to the student previously, can now become a positive and rewarding experience? How do we demonstrate that The Teacher can actually be someone who helps them to feel positive about themselves?

Another advantage in getting to know where our students are starting from is that, as well as discovering something about their attitudes to learning, we can learn something about their individual level of skill and knowledge. There may be things the student needs to learn before they can begin to address the outcomes specific to their programme of learning. For example, they may need to learn note-taking skills; or they may need to become familiar with the layout of a keyboard. They may need help in mastering certain social skills. Some types of challenging behaviour may arise simply as a result of the student not knowing what behaviour is appropriate to that particular situation. On the other hand, what they need to learn first may reside purely in the affective domain. They may need to learn to have trust – in you, the teacher, or in their own ability to achieve. Or they may need to learn the pleasure that follows achievement; that learning or mastering something new can make them feel good about themselves.

Let's have a look now at how one student teacher reflects on these issues in her journal after watching an experienced teacher with a class of 16 – 19 year olds.

February 22

My mentor's away ill today. I sat in instead with Gail who was taking a Kick Start class. I have to write 'taking' and not 'teaching' because I couldn't honestly see much teaching and learning going on. At least, not stuff the students were supposed to be learning. They were learning something, I suppose, but it was pretty counter-productive, in my opinion.

Actually, I really thought I was going to learn something in this class because everyone's always going on about how good Gail is at discipline – how she sorts the students out and they daren't give her any trouble. I could do with some of that! But anyway, this is what happened.

She was doing some basic psychology with them – a bit ironic, this – and she wanted them working in small groups, so she asked a couple of the girls to push some of the tables together. One of the boys – a little undersized shrimp of a lad who'd been joking about a bit – said something like, 'I'll do that, Miss. That's a man's job.' And G says, really loudly, 'Oh. It's a man's job, is it, Darren? Why's it a man's job?' And this gets the whole class's attention. So they're all smiling and watching what's going to happen. And Darren says, 'Well, because men are stronger aren't they.'

He's obviously trying to get her going, because he stands there grinning round at the class. They're all standing about while these girls move the tables. So anyway, G goes up to him – right up to him. She must be nearly six foot tall. And she towers over him and she looks down at him and she says, 'Men are bigger and stronger than women, are they Darren? Is that right?'

And all the class roars with laughter. They just fall about. And poor little Darren goes bright red. He tries to brazen it out for a second, but then he laughs lamely and starts looking in his bag. Actually, I wondered if he was going to cry. But he didn't.

I suppose I can see why she doesn't have much trouble with student behaviour. They'll all be pretty wary of her, even though they're laughing along. I don't suppose any of them wants to be next in line for a public humiliation. But this doesn't help me. I don't want to do it like that. I think those students were learning something I don't want mine to learn: that a teacher can pick up on anything you say and use it to humiliate you. She might have shut Darren up, but what's the main thing he's learnt in that lesson? And what's he likely to learn in the next one or the next, feeling how he must now about the teacher?

I don't think it was necessary to slap him down like that. He wasn't interrupting the others' learning. If I'd chosen to make any response to the 'man's job' thing, I'd have picked up on the offer of help – the positive bit – and let him join in with the two girls to shift a desk or two. And then thanked him. It was an opportunity to make him feel good about himself and his ability to be useful in the class – and G just let that go. She missed it and did the complete opposite instead. But I'm not going to tell her that! I wouldn't dare!

Close focus

How far do you agree with what this student teacher has to say about Gail's methods?

Do you agree with the journal writer's alternative way of handling the incident?

If you do not agree with her method or with Gail's, explain what your own approach would have been.

You may like to discuss this with your mentor or tutor, or use the questions as the basis for an entry in your reflective journal.

Starting with what is good

This chapter has been about starting points and how to identify them. Where we start from. Where our students are starting from. In the process we have, perhaps inevitably, focused upon problems: how to identify them and how to resolve them so that we can really get started on teaching and supporting student learning. Sometimes, however, in getting to know our students, we discover good places to start, as well as problems to resolve. A good illustration of this is found in the story of *Kes* by Barry Hines. You've probably read the book or seen the film. In this story a teacher of English in a Secondary school is able to use one teenage boy's consuming interest (in this case it is in the kestrel the boy is training) as a source of motivation for engaging with some of his schoolwork. This is an unusual starting point. For other students it might be their kind of music, or some film or television programme, or a sport, or a particular celebrity which will draw their interest. You might discover that a student has a particular talent, not obviously related to the subject you are teaching: impersonating someone famous, for example, or a high level of competence and confidence in ICT. These are all starting points. They all represent ways in which students can be helped to build their self-esteem and to find the experience of learning an enjoyable and non-threatening one.

Another way to start with what is good is to monitor our own attitude towards our students. This sort of metacognition – awareness of what we are thinking – or metamood – awareness of what we are feeling – is an important attribute for the teacher. If we are feeling fearful or resentful of a student, or cold and negative towards them, and are not sufficiently conscious of our feelings to conceal them, we may well let them show in our behaviour or our tone of voice, or simply in our body language. And this will serve only to reinforce the student's preconception that teachers are hostile, that they are an enemy to be confronted. Carl Rogers (1983) counsels that our students will learn most effectively when they have our 'unconditional positive regard'. This is a tall order. It's not always possible to control how we feel about our students. But we can cultivate the ability to remain aware of how we feel, so that we can be on our guard against communicating a negative attitude towards a student, which would discourage them from learning. 'Unconditional positive regard' may seem an impossible ideal. It provides, however, a good starting point, because it reminds us that we can and should behave in such a way as to make all our students feel valued for who and what they are. We may draw a line at accepting some of their behaviour or attitudes; but we should demonstrate that, as individuals, they are all valued, and all valued equally. Not only does this establish a model of acceptable and socially just behaviour, but it also demonstrates to the student that their negative construct of The Teacher may need re-examining. This is part of a set of values which lies at the heart of our professionalism. In the chapters which follow, we take a pragmatic approach to exploring various ways of putting these values into practice.

References

Rogers, C. (1983) *Freedom to Learn for the 80s*. Columbus, OH: Merrill

Wallace, S. (2001) *Teaching and Supporting Learning in FE: Meeting the FENTO Standards*. Exeter: Learning Matters

5 THE RULE BOOK

The end of law is, not to abolish and restrain, but to preserve and enlarge freedom.
John Locke, 1690

This chapter is about establishing rules for appropriate behaviour in order that learning may take place. It suggests ways in which appropriate behaviour can be agreed and monitored; and it examines some of the pitfalls which may follow from having too many rules or from enforcing them too rigidly.

The material in this chapter may be used for developing and reinforcing the following areas of skills and knowledge as set out in the FENTO Standards:

→ a1; a2; c1; d1; d3; e4; g1; g2; g3; h1; h2

General principles

It's impossible to talk to student teachers about the management of student behaviour without someone bringing up the issue of rules: what rules we should have in our classroom or our workshop, and how these should be enforced. And this is quite right; we do need to establish clear rules – what are now more commonly called *parameters of acceptable behaviour* – as part of creating an environment in which our students can feel safe and motivated to learn. What these parameters should be, and how we set them, will depend very much on the circumstances and on the nature of the learners.

Parveen

In order to arrive at some general principles, let's have a look at some extracts from a reflective journal written by Parveen, who has recently completed her Stage 3 FE teaching qualification, and is now at the beginning of her first full year of teaching.

October 3rd
I've had to take on another Intermediate group for a while because their teacher has gone on sick leave. M is taking over some of my Key Skills sessions to make room on my timetable for this lot. I say 'this lot' because, having met them this morning, I can't say I'm much looking forward to teaching them. Their other teacher only had them for a couple of weeks, but I think he must have just let them run riot.

> There were only four of them waiting outside when I got there. They got the computers on as soon as I'd unlocked the room and let them in. And I thought, oh good – they're keen. I waited a bit for the others to arrive (there are 20 on the register). I suppose I must have waited about 10 minutes; and then I thought I'd better make a start anyway. But I couldn't get these four to turn around and listen to what I was saying. And when I went round to look at what they were doing it was obvious they were just doing their own thing – messing about on the Internet, or playing games. Three more students drifted in, and then another two. The last two didn't even switch their machines on. The boy just started wheeling about the room on his chair (all the computer room chairs are on castors) making silly noises. The other one, the girl, just put her head down on her arms and appeared to go to sleep. I had several goes at getting their attention. I tried clapping my hands. I tried raising my voice. In the end I just switched all the machines off at the master switch, at which point there was a loud groan and yelps of protest from the seven who were logged on. They got quite aggressive. 'What you done that for?' and that sort of thing. I told them I needed them to listen carefully to my instructions before I'd switch back on again; and that if they weren't going to listen to what I had to say they may as well not be there. At this point one of them got up, picked up his bag (he'd never even taken his coat off), and made for the door. I shouted at him, 'Sit back down, now!' And he just stuck his chin out and said, 'Or else what?' and just walked out. I looked at the rest of them and it seemed as though they were all grinning at me, waiting to see what I'd do. All except the sleeping girl, who hadn't even looked up. Then the lad who was skating about on his chair said, 'Can we go for a break, Miss?' And they all took this up. 'We ought to have a break, Miss.' There were only 20 minutes to go before the end of the lesson, and I just thought, why not? It was a relief, really, to let them go.

Yes, it must have been. This can often be one of the difficulties of taking over someone else's class; that the standards of behaviour they expect don't tally with your own. Poor Parveen. But before we have a look at her own reflections about future strategy, let's examine what was happening and see whether we can come up with some strategies of our own.

Task

Read through the journal extract again and consider:

1. ***What could Parveen have done differently?***
2. ***What rules would it be useful to establish with this group?***
3. ***How would you prioritise those rules? (For example, if you could only establish one, which one would it be?)***

It would be a good idea to jot down your answers, or discuss them with a colleague or mentor, so that you can establish whether you agree or disagree with the ones suggested opposite.

Discussion

1. *What could Parveen have done differently?*

Let's look first of all at what Parveen herself has to say about this.

> **September 28th**
> I've been thinking about that awful class I had yesterday, and I've come to the conclusion that I started off all wrong. I shouldn't have waited for the rest of the class to turn up. It gave those first four the chance to start on something I didn't want them doing – and once they'd started, it was hard to stop them. I should have seized their attention before they even sat down, and briefed them on the first task before I switched on the master switch. Then when the next two lots of students arrived late, I could have briefed them as small groups, round my desk, before letting them sit down and switch their machines on. I'm sure that's the answer – to seize control from the first moment, to get the students all on task.

Do you agree? Would this strategy have worked, do you think? What about the student who put her head down and went to sleep, and the student who was playing about on his chair? Would the strategy Parveen proposes have ensured that these two stayed 'on task'?

It's worth spending a few minutes here to consider the behaviour of these two students. Anyone who has taught in FE is likely to have come across student behaviours such as these at some time or another. It would be a mistake, however, to disregard them as inevitable, or even as simply odd. Both of these students are quite clearly drawing attention to themselves. More, they are drawing attention to the fact that they, for one, aren't intending to do any work in this lesson. What both of them are doing by their behaviour is saying, 'Look! Look at me! I'm not doing this work!' *Now, why would they do that?* If they simply wanted to avoid working, wouldn't it be more advantageous not to draw the teacher's attention? What's going on here?

At the most basic level, we'd probably be safe in assuming that the main thing differentiating these two students from the other seven is that they don't want to work on the computers. The others, although they're ignoring the teacher and the set task, seem relatively interested, competent and confident as far as computers are concerned. It would be wise, therefore, for the teacher to consider the possibility that the behaviour of the two off-task students is an attempt to draw her attention because they need her help. This will not necessarily be true in every instance – rules of thumb are rarely that reliable – but it is always worth consideration. The chair boy may be avoiding sitting at the keyboard because his classmates will tease him if it becomes apparent he's no expert. It's far better for his image to show a bit of bravado by playing up the teacher. And then it'll seem as though he's not working just because he chooses not to, not because he doesn't know how.

Or perhaps the converse is true. Perhaps his computer skills are already so advanced that he's bored by anything this lesson might teach him. In either case, the teacher needs to find out; and the only way to do this is by engaging the student in dialogue.

Here, however, we might find that commonsense is contradicting theory. We are often told in books on psychology of education that we shouldn't reward attention-seekers by giving them what they want – that is, attention – since this will only provide positive reinforcement of that particular behaviour. That is, it will encourage the student to continue behaving in that way because they are learning that to do so gets them what they want; and what they want is attention. The theory is that the student must learn to ask for help in acceptable ways, rather than by acting disruptively or non-cooperatively. In many situations this would no doubt be sound advice, but the difficulties of applying it in Parveen's class are immediately evident. A pragmatic approach – speaking with the student and listening to what he has to say in an attempt to discover the reason for his resistance – would seem to be the most sensible way forward. In a chapter about rules, this is a useful one to bear in mind: that educational theory is only useful when it works in practice.

2. *What rules would it be useful to establish with this group?*

Again, let's look first here at what rules Parveen, after some reflection, decides she should establish.

September 28th (continued)

One thing's for certain: I'm going to have to impose a bit of order on that class or they're going to make things very difficult for me. They're going to have to learn some ground rules.

(i) Everyone must arrive on time.

(ii) Everyone must listen quietly to instructions before starting on the computers.

(iii) No-one must move from their place while the lesson is in progress.

(iv) No-one must speak without putting up their hand.

(v) No-one must shout out.

(vi) No-one to leave the room without my permission.

(vii) No-one to be working on anything other than the task I've set them.

(viii) No break (it's only a 50 minute lesson so they don't need one).

They've been getting away with things since the beginning of term. It's time to pull them up. I shall put these rules up on the board at the beginning of the next lesson, and let them know that anyone who breaks them is in trouble.

Goodness! It sounds as though they're not going to know what's hit them. Parveen is clearly determined to sort them out. To what extent does this set of rules match the one that you've drawn up? If Parveen were to ask you, what would be your professional judgement about her list? Like any good teacher, Parveen has two good reasons for wanting to establish the parameters of acceptable behaviour in her classroom. One is that it provides a better learning environment, and the other is that it makes her own task of supporting and encouraging student learning easier to carry out and more likely to succeed. It's important, when thinking about 'rules', to always bear these two purposes in mind. If you read that last journal extract again, you'll see that this teacher, in this particular instance, is taking a slightly one-sided view. Perhaps she's still feeling upset about what happened. But look at what she says:

> *I'm going to have to impose a bit of order on that class or they're going to make things very difficult for me.*

and

> *They've been getting away with things since the beginning of term. It's time to pull them up.*

We might think this sounds a little too much as though rules are being devised here as a punitive device; or at the best simply for the benefit of the teacher. Rules produced in this way are less likely to be successful than rules which are designed to support student learning. And this leads us on to our next question, which was:

3. *How would you prioritise those rules? (For example, if you could only establish one, which one would it be?)*

If I had to choose only one rule from Parveen's rather comprehensive list it would be number two:

> *Everyone must listen quietly to instructions before starting on the computers.*

The criterion I would apply in choosing this one would be precisely that which we have just been discussing: the promotion and support of student learning. If students are clear about the learning activity they are engaged in (and assuming that an activity has been chosen which will engage their interest and meet their needs), much of the rest will follow. Disruption is less likely; and, although it may not solve the problem of late arrivals, students will hopefully not be jostling to get out of the classroom before the end of the lesson.

Close focus

If this is not the rule you yourself would have prioritised, this doesn't mean that you're wrong and I'm right. What is important, however, is that you are able to give a rationale for your choice, and to explain and justify the criteria on which your decision was based. Your reflective journal is a good place to do this; or you may wish to expound your argument to a colleague or your mentor.

Parveen, meanwhile, is sticking to her eight rules. So let's have a look now at her journal entry for the next week and see how well they worked.

Task

As you read it through, make a note of what advice you would offer her.

October 4th

The Intermediate class again in the Computer Room. I made them wait outside this time – and I waited with them – until six of them had arrived, and then I unlocked the room and took them in. They did a lot of grumbling and moaning because I wouldn't switch the machines on until I'd written the rules up on the board. When I'd finished I told them to read them through and tell me if they had any questions. I couldn't get them completely quiet, and I don't know whether they all read them all. The only questions were: 'Are we allowed to breathe?' and 'Can we go now, Miss?' I gave out the sheets with their tasks on – keyboarding exercises to improve their speed – lots of groans from them – and only then did I switch the computers on. It immediately became apparent that no-one was doing the tasks and that they were just messing about. So I switched the machines off again. The boy who was scooting the chair about last week shouted 'Oi, Miss, out of order!' So I drew his attention to the rule about shouting out, and told him he would have to apologise. He said, 'No way.' When I insisted, he grabbed his bag and made for the door, with all the others roaring encouragement. I said, 'Sit back down. The rule is that everyone stays in their place.' – or something like that. I thought for a minute he was going to shove me out of the way, but instead he made this big show of stomping reluctantly back to his seat, playing to the audience. But it didn't feel like a victory to me at all. At least none of the others turned up. Six was just about manageable. But even so, I spent the whole time pulling them up for breaking every one of those rules, constantly having to remind them. It felt even worse than last time.

Discussion

So, what advice would you offer? It would probably include some or all of the following:

- It may be more productive to discuss and negotiate these kind of rules, rather than to simply impose them.
- The more rules you have to enforce, the less time you have for teaching and learning.
- One rule may be sufficient, if it's the right one.
- Your primary purpose, as a teacher, is to support student learning. The parameters you set should bear this in mind. Students remaining in their places, for

example, doesn't necessarily support student learning in situations where it may be useful for one student to help another.

- Avoid direct confrontation wherever possible. It can cause an already difficult situation to escalate.

What you will have jotted down, in fact, if you have spent some time over this exercise, is a set of rules about – yes – about making rules! They are guidelines which you can test and apply in the course of your own professional practice. They won't all be applicable, of course, in all situations; and, as your experience broadens, you may wish to amend and add to them.

Close focus

Let's take the last guideline on that list and look at it a little more closely. We have seen two examples of direct confrontation in Parveen's journal. They both arose over students leaving the room without permission. The first took place during her initial lesson with the class:

> **I told them I needed them to listen carefully to my instructions before I'd switch back on again; and that if they weren't going to listen to what I had to say they may as well not be there. At this point one of them got up, picked up his bag (he'd never even taken his coat off), and made for the door. I shouted at him, 'Sit back down, now!' And he just stuck his chin out and said, 'Or else what?' and just walked out.**

In her subsequent journal entries, Parveen doesn't get around to reflecting on what was going on here. So let's analyse it for her.

Question: *She describes herself twice here, speaking to the class and to the individual student. What is her manner of address?*
Answer: Well, she issues what appears to be an ultimatum to the whole class, which could be interpreted along the lines of, 'Do this or get out' ('if they weren't going to listen to what I had to say they may as well not be there.') When one of the students takes up the challenge and acts on this, she issues a direct order: 'Sit back down, now!'

Question: *Why was this manner of address – the ultimatum and the direct order – not a good idea under the circumstances?*
Answer: Because they didn't leave her any ground for retreat. This is illustrated very clearly when the departing student demands to know: 'Or else what?' Or else what, indeed? If the student is determined to get out of that door, there's very little that the teacher can do about it, within the parameters of her own professional conduct. Ultimata and orders are one way of trying to impose rules. They are not, however, necessarily the best or the only way. And the more rules we draw up, the more we impose upon ourselves the necessity of enforcing them. And there we are, spending far too much time issuing orders and ultimata.

Question: *So how could she have addressed this situation differently? What alternative form of words could she have used?*
Answer: Instead of saying, 'If you're not going to listen to what I have to say, you may as well not be here' she could have said:

- 'Let's have a look at what you should be able to do by the end of this lesson.'
- 'Is there anyone here who can already do this?'
- 'I wonder if all this noise means that some of you can do this already? I'd like those who can do this already to team up with someone who's still working on it, and give them a hand.'
- 'Let's find out from everybody what you'd like to have achieved by the end of this lesson. One at a time.'

All of these are worth a try. What they have in common is that they open up a dialogue with the students. The teacher isn't just issuing orders, but is creating the possibility of discovering why the students are behaving as they are.

Instead of saying, 'Sit back down, now!' she could have said:

- 'James? Where are you going?' (But she would have to have known his name for this, and I suspect that she didn't.)
- 'Where are you going?' (Notice the difference it makes when the name is missing. Immediately the question sounds more accusatory, less friendly.)
- 'I'd prefer it if you sat down. There are only a few minutes to go before the end of the lesson.'
- 'Listen. I'll need to talk to you about why you're leaving early.'
- 'Come on. Don't leave us. I need your help for this next bit.'

It may well be that none of these will prevent the student from leaving if he's determined to go. But all of them will give the correct message without raising the levels of anger and indignation and without creating a situation in which the teacher is seen to be directly disobeyed. And all of these suggestions are likely to be more effective if the student is addressed directly by name. You can demonstrate this for yourself now by prefixing a student's name to each of them, and trying both versions. The management of student behaviour is very much easier when you know your students' names. This is another rule to add to our list.

Negotiation

If we look at the language Parveen has used up to this point in her journal, we can see that she is operating within the assumption that rules are something which she decides upon, and then enforces by imposing them on the students. Look at some of the things she says:

> *I'm going to have to impose a bit of order.*

They're going to have to learn some ground rules.

I shall put these rules up on the board at the beginning of the next lesson, and let them know that anyone who breaks them is in trouble.

I spent the whole time pulling them up for breaking every one of those rules.

When Hazlitt wrote that 'Rules and models destroy genius and art', he was making a serious point which we can extend usefully to education. He was not advocating chaos and anarchy. What he was suggesting was that enthusiasm, creativity and initiative will not easily flourish in a situation where too many externally imposed rules allow only one pre-specified way of doing things. For example, in Parveen's class there may have been students who already possessed some of the skills she was trying to teach them. If the rule is that they have to go through all this again, they're likely to feel uncooperative and unenthusiastic. If the rule is that they all have to stay in their places, how can the more expert students use their skills to help their classmates – an activity that might well rekindle their motivation?

We all know that we have to have rules; but they're more likely to be adhered to if we've all agreed to them. Let's see what happens, then, when someone mentions this idea to Parveen and she begins to try it out.

October 11th

Third lesson with the dreaded group. I've put a lot of thought into what I should do. Yesterday I was talking to our section head about it, and I suddenly found myself getting quite upset. And then she said something really interesting. She said: 'Every single one of those students, if you could talk to them on their own, would admit there's a need for rules. Everyone feels safer if there are rules – as long as they see the sense in them. Why don't you get <u>them</u> involved – get them to suggest some rules?'

I don't think I'd have had the nerve to try this if the idea hadn't come from her. But she said it was quite a normal thing to do and that she always does it as a matter of course when she meets a new class. I think the trouble is I've just been sticking with what I learnt from my mentor last year. He was a bit of a stickler for discipline – which worked OK for him. So anyway, I let them all into the room this morning – there were ten here this time – and I didn't put the machines on, but waited until all the students were sitting down and looking towards me. And then I gave them a great big smile and said, 'OK. What rules would you like to have for this class? What rules would help you to work better?'

After we'd had a few of the inevitable witticisms such as, 'Leave early'; 'Not have to turn up if we don't want to'; 'You're not allowed to give us boring stuff to do'; 'James has to change his pants more often'; they actually began to come up with some sensible suggestions. The ones we agreed on in the end were:

- No-one is allowed to disturb anyone else if they're trying to work.
- If someone can already do the task I'm covering, they're allowed to go and help someone else who can't.

- If they all get the planned task done, they get to access the Internet until the end of the lesson.

Next thing I got them to do was to write up these rules, print them out, and put them at the front of their files. We also agreed to have two volunteers each week who would 'police' the rules. I don't know how well this will work in the long run – but the difference it made to today's lesson was amazing. They worked really well and there was a much friendlier atmosphere. I even felt they were beginning to like me.

Task

This sounds like a happy ending. But in fact, of course, it's not. It's a beginning – a new start – and it's by no means certain that Parveen and her class will live happily ever after. But she has taken a step towards getting the students to engage with their learning. She will no doubt have to take others. There are some indications in this last journal entry (and in the earlier ones, too) as to what some of these might be. Read through the entries again and see whether you can identify at least two issues which Parveen will need to address in her future planning for this class.

Discussion

As far as most of the students are concerned, their motivation for the subject is not in doubt. They want to work on the computers. We know this because Parveen tells us that 'They did a lot of grumbling and moaning because I wouldn't switch the machines on.'

But they seem very poorly motivated to carry out the tasks which she sets them. The impression that emerges is that they don't find these tasks very interesting. We know this because one of the rules they suggest is that 'You're not allowed to give us boring stuff to do.'

Now, we could argue that this is the equivalent of an aspiring pianist complaining about having to practise their scales: a repetitive but nevertheless essential step in achieving competence. We also know that 'It's boring!' is the eternal lament of the young. However, in this case, we have some evidence which indicates that some of the students may feel bored simply because they are already familiar with, and able to carry out, the tasks and procedures she is covering in her lesson plans. Otherwise why would they have come up with the rule 'If someone can already do the task I'm covering, they're allowed to go and help someone else who can't?'

One of the issues that Parveen is going to need to address, therefore, is differentiation – setting differentiated tasks and goals appropriate to the individual student's current needs. She will also need to look at ways to engage students' enthusiasm for the tasks she sets them. This may involve revising or extending her range of teaching methods, or finding ways to illustrate to the students the relevance of what they are learning to their own aspirations and goals. This, in turn, will mean getting to know the individual students, and devising activities which allow her to work with them on a one-to-one basis so that she can engage with them and listen to what they have to say. Agreeing rules with your students is only the first step. Whether you can continue to work together within those rules will depend on how effectively you plan to meet their needs; and this in turn usually comes down to how well you know your students. The centrality of the teacher–student relationship in establishing the positive behaviour of students is a theme we shall keep coming back to.

Parveen will also have to address the issue of low attendance (only about half of the students on the register seem to be turning up), and to investigate the needs of the boy in the chair and the sleeping girl.

Close focus

The final sentence of Parveen's last entry reads:

I even felt they were beginning to like me.

How important a factor do you consider this to be in the context of setting parameters to student behaviour? This is an issue which you might like to reflect on in your journal.

Implementing the rules of others

The parameters governing behaviour in our classrooms and workshops and other environments in which we teach extend beyond those set by ourselves and our students. First of all there are the rules and regulations set by the institution in which we work. These will cover behaviour – both that of the students and our own – and other issues such as health and safety. Some of the regulations may seem comparatively minor. For example, it may be a college rule that no food or drink is allowed in the classroom. Working as you are, in a professional context and within a set of professional values, it is part of your professional responsibility to uphold these rules, *even if you don't personally consider them important.* This also means not trivialising them; not saying for example, 'I know it's a stupid rule, but …'

Or 'If it was up to me I'd let you … eat your sandwiches off your computer keyboard,' or whatever. This is part of what the FENTO requirement for teachers to 'conform to agreed codes of professional practice' is about.

Secondly, of course, there is the law of the land. If a student comes to you and says, 'I need to tell you something. Do you promise not to say anything to anybody?' – beware! You don't have the immunity of a doctor or a priest, who can claim ethical reasons for maintaining confidentiality. If, having extracted a promise of silence from you, a student tells you he's shot his grandma, you become an accessory after the fact unless you report it to the police. The best response to such a request for confidentiality is to say: 'If there's something you want to talk about, of course I'm willing to listen. But I can't promise to keep it confidential because there may be something in what you tell me which I need to pass on, in your interests or in mine.'

Summary

- Know your students. Listen to them. Learn their names.
- The test of a rule's usefulness is whether it supports student learning.
- Rules are easier to implement if students share ownership of them.
- Having too many rules to enforce can be counter-productive.
- Theory is only useful if it works in practice.

6 GREAT EXPECTATIONS

Possunt, quia posse videntur (They can because they think they can).
Virgil

This chapter is about how our expectations of our students – and our students' expectations of themselves – can influence their willingness and ability to learn. It suggests ways in which these preconceptions can be challenged, and examines strategies for raising students' self-esteem and helping them to set positive, achievable goals.

The materials in this chapter may be used for developing and reinforcing the following areas of skills and knowledge as set out in the FENTO Standards:

→ a1; a2; b3; c1; c2; c3; d1; d3; e2; e4; f2; g1; g2; h1

They also address the personal attributes listed by FENTO as desirable in an FE teacher.

It's not a battle!

When Nelson sent a signal to his fleet before the Battle of Trafalgar '*England expects that every man will do his duty*', was he reminding the crews to obey orders – *behave the way you're supposed to, or else* – or was he letting them know that he had absolute faith in their courage and ability; that he and all England *knew* that these sailors and their officers would do their duty? I prefer to think it was the latter. Shipboard discipline may have been draconian, but in this instance Nelson probably knew that he could get the best out of these people by speaking to them as though they were already heroes. There's something we can learn here, and apply to our own much smaller battles, which are often about gaining students' attention, getting them to recognise the satisfaction to be gained from learning and achieving, and convincing them that there's more reward in learning than there is in disruption and challenging behaviour. Our battles can sometimes even be with ourselves when, for instance, we have to go in there and face a class whose behaviour we feel has slipped beyond our control.

We are using the metaphor of a battle here because that's sometimes what it can feel like when we're trying to motivate students and manage their behaviour. However, it's a metaphor we should beware of internalising as a model for our professional practice! Teaching and supporting learning is not, and should not be, a battle between the teacher the students. The trouble is, it can sometimes feel like one. This is probably because so many of our students do seem to see it this way; in Chapter 3 we saw how Parveen, when she began drawing up rules for student behaviour, was also in a sense drawing up battle lines, which only made her task even more difficult.

Gloria

Let's have a look at another teacher now. Gloria is on a part-time contract, teaching Health and Social Care. This is her first year of teaching, and she has just begun working towards her Stage 2 qualification. She's already teaching ten hours a week when she receives a call from her college asking if she will also come in and take over a Key Skills Communication class for a few weeks. Having agreed to do this, she reflects on what happens next in the journal she's keeping as part of her Stage 2 teacher training programme.

Task

Read through the journal entry below and consider the following questions:

1. ***At what point, if any, during this scenario could Gloria have taken steps to improve her situation?***
2. ***What, specifically, was she frightened of? What's the worst that could happen?***
3. ***How would you interpret the student behaviour that Gloria saw as she entered the room? What do you think this behaviour is communicating?***
4. ***What are the possible reasons for the students feeling like this?***

December 3rd – midnight

Can't sleep. Decided to write this up – try to decide whether I'm getting it all out of proportion. I said I'd take over the Key Skills class, partly for the experience, and partly because I want to appear willing, in case a full-time post comes up. All I knew was that they were Construction trainees, thirteen of them, all male, and the person who normally taught them Communications was off sick. The class was on the top floor of J Block, four flights up. I was walking up the stairs with the register and the work sheets when I passed the Section Head of Construction coming down. He said, as he walked past me: 'Have you come in to do the Key Skills? They're all up there waiting for you. Complete waste of time, and they know it is. I won't tell you what they did to the last bloke. Won't be seeing him again. I hope you last a bit longer. Doubt it, though.'

I suddenly felt frightened. My heart started banging away, and it wasn't just those stairs. I was thinking, 'Oh no. Have I brought the right sort of work for them? What's going to happen when I walk in? What if they make me look stupid as soon as I walk in – how am I going to spend the next hour and a half with them? What did they do to their last teacher? Oh no. What did they do to their last teacher?'

When I came to the bottom of the last flight of stairs, I could hear them. They were laughing and shouting and swearing. And I just wanted to drop the register and run. When I got to the top of that last flight I knew I should stop for a minute and get my breath back so that I didn't go in there all red in the face and breathless. But I also knew that if I hesitated for one moment, I wouldn't be able to make myself do it. I'd just turn and run. So I pushed open the door and went in. Twelve big lads lounging about at three rows of tables, bags slung everywhere, some on the tables being used as pillows, some on the floor. One lad standing on the windowsill rattling at the top window. When I stepped into the room and stopped, some of them noticed right away and shouted out to the others who were still yelling and laughing. 'Ay-up, lads. She's here. Look who's here.' There was one moment of silence in which all their eyes turned to me – to weigh me up, I suppose. And I said, 'Good morning. My name is —' And there was this twanging sound like a bouncing spring – and they all just started falling about laughing. One of them had a steel ruler wedged under the edge of the table – I spotted it when he twanged it again. Renewed roars of laughter. And the laughter was out of all proportion to the joke. That's the thing. It was a feeble joke, even the first time. So why did they find it so bloody funny? And there was I, two paces into the room, red in the face and out of breath, desperately thinking: What do I do? What do I do?

Discussion

A good question. What *does* she do? We'll be coming back to that in some detail later. For the moment let's have a look at our questions, which focus on what has happened up to this point.

1. *At what point, if any, during this scenario could Gloria have taken steps to improve her situation?*

Most of us would probably be inclined to say that 'taking steps' was one of her mistakes. She'd have felt less flustered if she'd chosen to take the lift! But leaving that sort of advice aside, what could she have done? Was there an opportunity she missed?

I think there was. I think she could have used that encounter on the stairs to her advantage, and asked – even insisted – that the Section Head go up with her and introduce her to the class. If he was behaving professionally, instead of trying to wind her up, he would have offered to do this as a matter of courtesy, both to her and to the students. This would have achieved several things. It would have given Gloria the opportunity to find out more practical information about the class as she and he walked up together; it would have allowed her to see how he interacted with the students and whether there was anything in his approach that she could use; and it would have allowed her to enter the classroom initially as an observer for those first few crucial minutes while he was, nominally, in charge. Of course, he might have refused to do it, but it would certainly have been worth a try. One thing that Gloria's situation illustrates very clearly is the need for newly-appointed or inexperienced teachers to have the support of a mentor. For an inexperienced teacher to be confronted by a 'difficult' or challenging class without first being given the opportunity to see how a more experienced teacher manages them, is both unfair and unproductive. And indeed, the same principle applies for student teachers engaged in teaching practice at an FE college. There is nothing to be gained, in terms of either student or teacher learning, by setting them in front of badly behaved students unless they've had the opportunity to see how an experienced teacher handles it. This provides them at least with a model of what does, or does not, work. It provides a starting point for reflection without crushing their confidence and enthusiasm. They – you, perhaps – have a right to ask for this kind of support. Gloria's Section Head, by the sound of it, couldn't care less about any of that. And that's a shame. But we've all met him, at some time, in some guise or another.

2. *What, specifically, was she frightened of? What's the worst that could happen?*

This is always a useful question – difficult to answer at the time, perhaps, but important to reflect upon after the panic has subsided. What Gloria fears here is what any of us would fear in such a situation: that's she's walking into a situation that she won't be able to control; that the students are hostile and she will be the target of that hostility; that she won't be able to maintain her professional role – that her professional persona will disintegrate and she'll be reduced to the status of a victim who flees from the room or starts crying. For most of us, our self-esteem is partially dependent on our ability to carry out our professional role. Faith in this ability to carry out our role is very important to the way we feel about ourselves. Any threat to it is a very big deal. That's why Gloria, although she's not, as far as she knows, in any physical danger, is reacting with such a powerful fight or flight response. She feels threatened. She wants to run away. And it's made worse for her by the vague, unspecified dangers which the Section Head has gleefully hinted at:

> *I won't tell you what they did to the last bloke. Won't be seeing him again. I hope you last a bit longer. Doubt it, though.*

So there's this additional threat, although she has no idea of its exact nature. All she knows is that, if she's to conform to her own ideal of professional behaviour, she has to go in there and face it. Poor Gloria. We all know it's nerve-racking enough to face an unfamiliar group of students for the first time, without being told vague horror stories about them first.

But what *is* the worst that can happen? If we're realistic, the worst that can happen is that her personal and professional confidence will receive a knock, and she will feel humiliated or made to look silly in front of thirteen teenage boys. Bad enough, you might say. But then no-one ever said that teaching was easy. The worst thing, in other words, is to encounter the class or the situation which brings you up against the limits of your own professional or personal ability to cope. Seen in this light, it may not be an entirely negative thing. We all do have limits. Part of being a professional is to be clear about where those limits are. We do this by reflecting on our experience and learning from it. We need to know our weaknesses as well as our strengths. Our weaknesses, or our areas for professional development, will change over time. But it's unlikely we'll ever all be excellent at everything. If we drive ourselves towards that goal we are letting ourselves in for a lot of stress and a sense of failure. In Chapter 1 we saw how some aspects of student behaviour and motivation can be attributed to factors outside the teacher's control. We should always keep this in mind. In Gloria's case there is a possibility that a disastrous encounter with these students might imply something other than a failure on her part. And even if it is a failure on her part, then at least she has learnt something about her current limitations and can plan her professional development accordingly.

3. *How would you interpret the student behaviour that Gloria saw as she entered the room? What do you think this behaviour is communicating?*
4. *What are the possible reasons for the students feeling like this?*

I'm going to take these two questions together, because it's likely that in considering your answers you've already linked the two. First of all it would be fair to guess that they're communicating a lack of interest in the subject they find themselves timetabled for – the subject Gloria's been brought in to teach them – Key Skills Communication. Given the Section Head's attitude, this is hardly surprising. He's already admitted he doesn't see the point of it; and this attitude may well have communicated itself to the students. In any case, as far as they're concerned, they're in college to learn about Construction, and are probably of the view that anything else is a waste of time. We've also had a strong hint that their previous teacher found them too much to cope with. If this is so, the group has learnt that challenging behaviour works quite well at getting rid of the teacher and is therefore an effective way of avoiding having to do the subject. However, as we've learnt from Chapters 3 and 4, this sort of student behaviour can be communicating other things, too. Perhaps some of them are intimidated by the subject, and are, under all the bravado, feeling as nervous as Gloria is that something is going to be demanded of them here that is beyond their capabilities; that they are going to be made to look foolish. Disruption may be their only way to stop this lesson happening. It's possible, too, that some of them may feel disturbed by what happened to the previous teacher. They may be uncomfortable with the idea that they were able to defeat the person who was supposed to be 'in charge'. This may have made them feel insecure or angry.

One thing is certain. This behaviour is not communicating any personal animus towards Gloria. How could it? They have never met her before. They don't know what sort of a person she is, nor what sort of a teacher she is. When they twang the ruler in order to make fun of her, and roar with laughter at her discomposure, it's not aimed at her specifically, but at the idea of 'Teacher'; or perhaps, in this case, the idea of 'Communication Teacher'. In other words they illustrate very nicely the tendency we discussed in Chapter 3 for students to superimpose on any teacher the construct of Teacher-as-Villain which they have built out of their negative experiences. This is why she recognises, even in her panic, that the laughter is out of proportion to the joke. The students' intent is to get at the Teacher. The joke is therefore just an excuse for them to laugh. It's an act of aggression, but it's not personal.

Would Gloria derive any comfort from understanding all this at the point at which it's happening? Perhaps. But it's hard to feel philosophical when you're also feeling frightened and being laughed at. So it would be expecting too much of anyone, I think, to feel perfectly comfortable in this situation. The crucial thing, however, will be how she answers her own question: 'What do I do?'

We left her standing just inside the classroom, holding her register and her folder of work, out of breath from the stairs, listening to a group of students roaring with laughter at her expense. We're going to step now into the realms of science fiction and give Gloria two alternative futures with this class. The future she inhabits will depend on what she does next. This is the place at which the road forks. Let's say straight away, though, that if she takes the wrong fork this time and finds herself in the more difficult version of her future, there'll always be another fork – another chance to rescue the situation. That, after all, is what teaching and learning is like.

Task

So, here are the next pages of Gloria's journal in one of those two futures. Read them through carefully and consider what general guidelines we might draw from them about managing difficult behaviour and supporting student learning.

'What do I do?' So I took a deep breath and grinned. A great big grin that crinkled up my eyes as though I really meant it. And I nodded at the lad with the steel ruler and made a mock bow. One of them shouted at him, 'She fancies you, Waheed!' And there was a bit of whistling. I walked to the table at the front, still grinning. I was trying to act as though I really wanted to be there. As though there was nowhere else I'd rather be. As though I'd been looking forward to this all week, and it was every bit as wonderful as I'd hoped it would be. This was pure survival. It seemed the only way to go. And I honestly think I'd have won an Oscar for it in a film. I put my stuff down and called to the lad on the windowsill, 'Thanks! Can you open the next one along as well? It's a bit stuffy in here.' Some more cat calls, but window boy seemed to like the attention. He opened the other top window and then jumped down and sat at his table (Thank goodness! Thank goodness!). I leaned against the table at the front and smiled round at them until I'd made eye contact with them all – except for Waheed, who was twanging away at his ruler. But it wasn't getting much of a laugh any more. It was probably getting on everybody else's nerves as much as it was on mine. And then one of them told him to 'Shut the **** up,' and then added, 'Whoops. Sorry, Miss.' Which got a bit of a laugh – but they were generally quietening down, the longer I stood there smiling, saying nothing. One of them shouted, 'What's she smiling at?' And then to me, 'What you smiling at?'

I said, 'I'll tell you in a minute. When you're all quiet.'

There was still a bit of sniggering and whispering to each other – looking at me out of the corner of their eyes – still trying to make me feel uncomfortable – and succeeding, though I wouldn't let them know it.

It was no good waiting for absolute quiet – I don't think that would've happened. So when it was about as quiet as I thought it would get, I said, 'I've been looking forward to meeting you lot. Mr P [the Section Head]'s been telling me all about you.'

Groans. Shouts. 'What's he said, Miss?' 'Go on. What's he said?'

'Some good things. But one of the things he said was you didn't like Communication.'

Groans again. 'Waste of time', 'Rubbish' – and much worse. But there were quite a few of them wanting to know what good things he's said. I suppose that's human nature. And I think that was what I was banking on. But it was a bit tricky, because the horrible man hadn't said anything good about them at all. Anyway, I sort of struck a deal with them. I said that if they'd tell me, clearly and honestly, why they didn't like Communication, then I'd tell them all the good things Mr P had said about them.

It got really interesting then. I actually forgot I was nervous of them, and started enjoying it. Some of them were even putting their hand up when they wanted to say something – wonderful how eleven years of schooling leaves its mark! I listed the main points they made on the flip chart. They included all the predictable things like:

Boring
Pointless
Takes up time they could be spending on other things
Won't ever be any use to them
And so on

I told them I was going to take it away and turn it into a sort of contract with them for next week – whereby if I could demonstrate to them that they were misjudging the subject, then they'd agree to revise their opinion of it. They jeered a bit at that – but it didn't matter because we were moving things forward and I still had most of their attention most of the time.

I said, 'OK. So do you want to hear some nice things about yourselves?' And I made out that Mr P had said they were a very promising bunch, and that they were nice lads, and they had a good sense of humour.

Too bad if they ask him about this. It does no harm. And if he denies it – well – they'll just think he's pretending to be hard, but that really he praises them behind their backs. It was funny, though, because I could tell from their comments that they didn't really like him very much.

When I felt I'd really had enough of Waheed and his steel ruler, I said, 'Do you play any other instruments, Waheed?' They all laughed. And it was me who'd cracked the joke. That felt like a small victory of sorts.

Discussion

So is there anything we can generalise from this? Are there any guidelines, any rules of thumb we might draw from this version of Gloria's future? It goes without saying that we can't draw any hard and fast rules. What works in one situation with one particular group of students won't necessarily succeed in similar circumstances or with a different group. One of the things that makes dealing with this kind of behaviour challenging is that we often have to play it by ear. There is no foolproof set of procedures. Nevertheless, there are a number of general guidelines which we can bear in mind to help us; and Gloria's journal pages illustrate these for us.

✓ Gloria acts as though she's pleased to be there. She acts as though she was expecting to enjoy meeting the students and enjoy the lesson with them. She gives no indication from her manner that she expects any trouble from them. Acting as though we are confident can, as cognitive psychologists will tell you, make us actually feel more confident. If we adopt the body language and expression of a confident person the feeling of confidence will often follow. One of the most obvious ways in which this works is that it affects how others respond to us. In this case, Gloria's students are responding to an apparently confident teacher, one who seems pleased to be with them. This response of theirs, in turn, reinforces her confidence. In this way the relationship between the teacher and students is moving in a positive direction. If, on the other hand, Gloria had let her fear and reluctance become apparent, the students would probably have responded with a similar hostile negativity, which would exacerbate Gloria's lack of confidence.

✓ What Gloria succeeds in doing here is convincing the students that she has positive expectations of them. She even, for good measure, makes up a story about their Section Head having positive expectations of them, too. If you look at how she deals with the student on the windowsill, you see that she chooses to attribute a helpful motive to his being up there. He gets the message that she sees him not as a disruptive student, but as a helpful student who is trying to open the window so that the classroom feels less stuffy. This is often worth a gamble. The student must then choose which role to adopt – helpful or disruptive. But at least he has a choice. He has not been boxed into the role of disruptive student from the start and therefore needn't feel compelled to play up to it. Similarly, Gloria puts the best possible construction on the classroom banter. When the students shout, 'What's she smiling at?' and 'What you smiling at?' she chooses not to interpret this as rude or aggressive, but as a genuine question which she promises to answer. She is signalling to the students that she expects to like them, and that they are living up to her expectations.

✓ She is also able to use humour to help defuse aggression and to indicate that they are all – students and teacher – on the same side. When she asks Waheed whether he plays any other instruments, she's not only telling him in a nonaggressive way that they're all a bit bored now with the noise he's making; she's also subtly altering the dynamics in that room. For a moment it is no longer students *v.* teacher, but everyone irritated by the noise Waheed is making *v.* Waheed. The students laugh at her joke, rather than at the twang of the ruler. In this way she brings peer pressure to bear rather than using direct confrontation. She is able to signal her expectation of an orderly working environment and a friendly working atmosphere without having to get angry or unfriendly. Did you notice, also, that she capitalised on the noisy reception they gave her by taking the opportunity to memorise Waheed's name? She was then able to play this card later for maximum impact.

✓ Gloria starts by finding out what the students' expectations are. She asks for their views about the subject, and validates their responses by showing that she takes them seriously. In this way, she signals that they are in this together; that there is room for negotiation; that this is not a student *v.* teacher situation, but a team effort to which both teacher and students can contribute.

✓ Taken together, the various aspects of Gloria's behaviour make it very difficult for the students to continue superimposing the Teacher-as-Villain construct on her. In other words, she challenges their own expectations and – with luck – encourages them to rethink.

To summarise then: the strategies that Gloria is using here are

- acting confidently and appearing pleased to be teaching the class;
- making the students feel that she and others have good expectations of them;
- putting the best possible interpretation on students' behaviour and playing things down;
- using humour to defuse hostility;
- discussing the students' own views and expectations;
- challenging the Teacher-as-Enemy stereotype;
- quickly learning some names.

We must beware, of course, of taking a sentimental Hollywood approach to this. The 'Dynamic Teacher Wins Over Troublesome Class' scenario is rarely as simple as that in real life. Gloria's strategy, in this version of events, has proved successful in this particular class on this particular day. This is not to say that the strategy would be foolproof for every group of students, nor that this class will be easy to face next time she meets them. What we can take from this account are ideas and guidelines that may help us when we find ourselves facing similarly challenging situations. The extent to which these strategies work in any instance will depend on many factors; but whether they succeed or fail, they provide a useful starting point for reflection.

Close focus

Some of Gloria's strategies were high risk. You might like to discuss, in your journal or with your mentor:

- ***the Health and Safety implications of the way Gloria dealt with the student on the windowsill;***
- ***the ethical implications of pretending to the students that the Section Head had spoken well of them;***
- ***the acceptability of a joke made at one student's expense.***

We've seen one version of Gloria's future. Let's put her back in the doorway now and look at an alternative version of what might have happened.

Task

Read Gloria's account of this alternative version of the same lesson, and consider the following questions.

1. ***At what point did things begin going wrong?***
2. ***Can you identify any occasions on which there was an opportunity to 'rescue' the situation?***

'What do I do?' So I took a deep breath and said, 'Alright now. Settle down. And you,' to the boy with the steel ruler, 'put that away. And you,' to the boy on the windowsill, 'get down from there before you fall. Get down, now.'

He waved his arms about and did a good impression of someone losing their balance. Then he flapped his arms as though he was going to fly. The others were all hooting and shouting. I slammed my folder and the register down on the nearest table and shouted, 'I said get down. Now.' He jumped down and half landed on one of the other boys and they started a bit of a scuffle. The steel ruler twanged again, like a sound effect, and the ones who weren't watching the 'fight' laughed with delight. So I said, 'Give me that!' He meekly held out the ruler towards me and then as I went to grasp it, he snatched it away, slipped it under the table top and twanged it again. I said, 'Yes. Very funny. I suppose you've heard the saying, Small things amuse small minds.'

They leapt on this, of course. Lots of innuendo about 'small things'. Lots of laughing and pointing. I should have seen it coming, I suppose. But I was distracted by this scuffle going on. It wasn't a fight really, because it wasn't serious. But it was distracting everyone's attention and obviously I couldn't let it go. So I said, 'Come on. Settle down. Stop that. It's like being with a bunch of animals.' Then, of course, the animal noises started. I was thinking, 'Oh no. If anyone hears this going on they're going to think I'm a complete loser. They'll never give me a full-time job.' And I found myself really hating these students for putting me through this. What had I ever done to them?

When that boy twanged the ruler again it was the last straw. I said, 'Here! Give that to me! Now!'

He put it behind his back, grinning.

I said, 'Now! Or else!'

The boy behind him said, 'Or else what?' And someone else made that silly surprised exclamation: 'Ooooo!'

So I said, 'Or else you can get out!'

Then lots of them joined in with this 'Oooooo!' noise. I shouted at them, 'Just settle down!' The scuffle was still going on, and I couldn't tell now whether it was still in fun. Then I glanced in the other direction and saw that a couple of them had picked up my file and the register. They were writing in the register – they seemed to be making alterations in it and laughing and showing it to the table behind them. I said, 'Give it to me.' And then someone shouted, 'Go on. She wants you to give it to her.' Roars of laughter. I couldn't let this go. So I told the boy who'd shouted to get out. He didn't budge. And then I just lost it. I shouted at the top of my voice, 'Get out!' But they all just laughed. I made a grab for the register and it tore in half. They thought this was hilarious. 'Look what you done now, Miss!'

'Well that's about what you deserve. Half a register – for a bunch of half-wits. If you think I'm going to waste my time with you, you've got another think coming.' And I walked out. I still can't believe I did it. I just walked out. With my half of the register. I'd never even got as far as the teacher's table. Why should I put up with that sort of thing? Whatever they paid me, it still wouldn't be worth it.

Discussion

And so Gloria walks out. The trouble is, this makes it very difficult to walk back in again, and most teachers' contracts will require them to do just that. This version of events is not a comfortable one to read, but there's a great deal to be learned from it. Let's take our first question.

1. *At what point did things begin going wrong?*

I don't think they were destined to go wrong from the start. Gloria's firm approach – her initial efforts to establish order by asking the student to get down from the windowsill and the other to stop playing with the ruler – was a perfectly reasonable one. Many of us would have started off that way. She was laying her ground rules for acceptable behaviour and acting appropriately in her role as classroom manager. I think the point at which it began to go wrong was when she responded to the boy on the windowsill like this:

> *I slammed my folder and the register down on the nearest table and shouted, 'I said get down. Now.'*

This display of anger was, I think, a mistake. Showing that you are angry can send the wrong signals. Someone who feels completely in control of a situation doesn't usually need to flare up with anger. Gloria therefore weakens her position by getting angry at this point – within only a few minutes of meeting the group. She also escalates the confrontation. There was still room at this point to respond to his bird imitations with a long-suffering smile, a few nods, and a quiet, 'Come on.'

2. *Can you identify any occasions on which there was an opportunity to 'rescue' the situation?*

The reality is that every minute Gloria spends in that classroom presents an opportunity to rescue the situation. Until she storms out. Then it becomes very difficult to rescue indeed.

As the seconds ticked by, however, she only succeeded in making the situation worse and worse. Here are some of the mistakes and misjudgements you are likely to have identified.

✗ She makes it clear to the students that she doesn't like being with them.

✗ She makes it clear that she has low expectations of them.

✗ She turns every incident into a confrontation.

✗ She causes every confrontation to escalate, instead of playing it down or defusing it.

✗ She interprets all student behaviour as hostile.

✗ She makes a big deal out of every small incident (instead of addressing the potentially serious issue of a scuffle that may be turning into a fight).

✗ She doesn't choose her words carefully, with the result that she fuels the students' enjoyment of innuendo.

✗ She displays no sense of humour, nor any other trait that would dispose the students to like her.

Of these two alternative scenarios, I would prefer to think that Gloria stepped into the first. But even if she stepped into the second, there would be a great deal she could learn from the experience if she took the time to analyse and reflect.

Summary

We began this chapter with a metaphor about battles. We could interpret Gloria's two alternative realities as a battle won and a battle lost. The first a victory, the second a defeat. But the battle isn't between the teacher and the students. If the students don't learn and don't find their learning worthwhile, then everyone loses. The battle – if we're going to call it that – is for the hearts and minds of the students. It is one that is fought to motivate them and to develop their potential. And one of the ways we can win it is to let them know that we have great expectations of them; not necessarily in the sense of high achievement, but rather an expectation that we can enjoy working together towards whatever goals are appropriate to them.

7 BREAKING OUT

Discovery consists of seeing what everybody has seen and thinking what nobody has thought.
Albert von Szent-Gyorgyi, 1962

This chapter is about thinking 'outside the box'. First it examines a range of currently accepted theories of learning, and tries them out on familiar classroom situations. In this way it illustrates and discusses their usefulness and their limitations in helping us to better understand how students may be motivated and positive behaviour encouraged. It then goes on to demonstrate how teachers themselves can theorise from their own experience, and how such theorising may help them to develop the strategies which work most effectively for their students.

The material in this chapter may be used for developing and reinforcing the following areas of skills and knowledge as set out in the FENTO Standards:

→ d1; d2; d3; d4; e4; f2; g1; g2; g3; h1; h2

Theories of learning

If we turn to the textbooks on learning theory to try to understand why our students are confrontational or appear disinclined to engage with their college work, we will find no shortage of theoretical answers and advice. Often this can help us to understand why a student or students are behaving in a certain way, but it doesn't always help us to understand what we can do about it in terms of specific, realistic, day-to-day strategies. In the first part of this chapter, we're going to have a look at three learning theorists whose work has informed much recent and current thinking in education. Broadly speaking, they approach an individual's readiness or willingness to learn as a psychological issue. In Chapter 1 we saw that there may be other factors – historical, practical, sociological and economic – which underlie some of the difficult situations which FE teachers are faced with in the classroom and the workshop. In the process of considering what the learning theorists have to say, we should keep this wider context in mind. Real life is rarely as clear cut as text-book answers might suggest. No theory, however inspired, will work for every situation, every time. When we confront a difficult situation with our students – whether it be lack of motivation or inappropriate behaviour – the causes are likely to be complex. That is why finding the answer is not always easy.

According to Maslow (1954), part of the answer may be found by taking into consideration what he would term our students' 'hierarchy of needs'. As human beings, our more basic needs, such as the need for comfort or for safety, must be met before we can turn our attention to satisfying our higher-order needs. Achieving our potential through learning is one of these higher-order needs. Therefore, Maslow would argue, if a student is cold, or uncomfortable, or frightened or has certain worries on their mind, they won't be able to turn their attention to learning, until these lower-order needs are met. This hierarchy of needs is usually represented as a pyramid, with very basic physiological needs forming the broad base, and with self-actualisation at the apex. In a simplified version, it would look something like this.

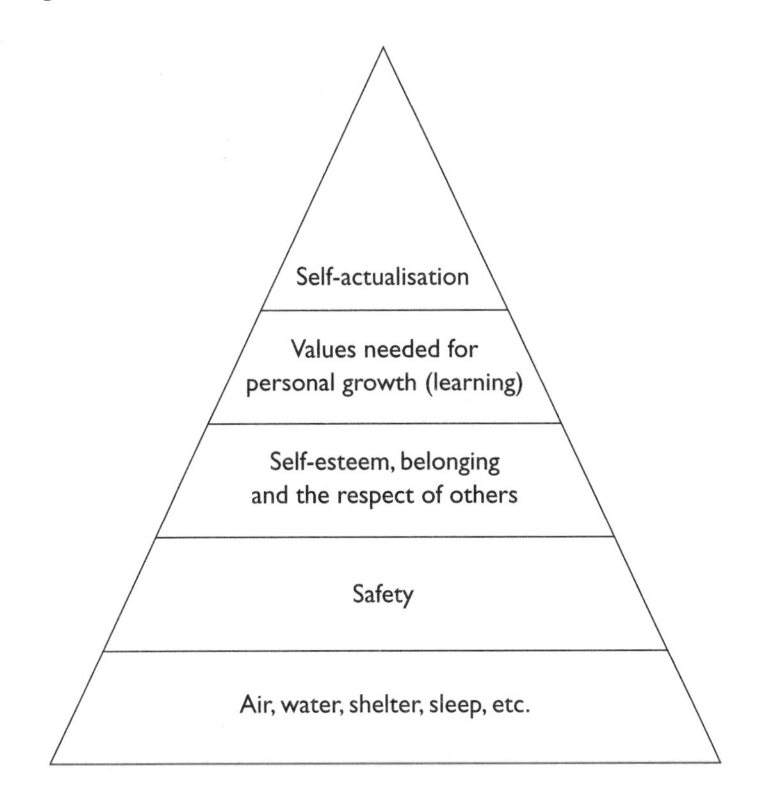

On a very basic level, then, this would mean that in a chilly classroom our best first step towards getting the students to attend to their learning will be to turn on the radiators. Any other strategy we use – such as encouragement, or devising fascinating activities for them to do – will have only limited success until their basic need for a tolerable temperature to work in is met.

Now, let's consider this for a moment in the light of what we have read in Chapter 1. If Maslow is right and a sense of self-worth or the feeling that we are valued by others is a prerequisite for our receptivity to learning, then we can see why students who fared badly in school, who associate education with personal failure or who feel they are being 'fobbed off' with a training that will never lead to real employment, would appear unwilling or unready to learn. Similarly, we can see why, if students are afraid that their inability or ignorance will be exposed, or if they're afraid of mockery from their peers or admonishment from their teacher, that fear – the feeling that they are not safe – will operate to block their co-operation and engagement with their learning. What is immediately apparent here is that there is only so much that the teacher can do to remedy this. Maslow's theory is helpful in explaining why some students are disinclined to learn; but if their fear or lack of self-esteem owes some of its origins to factors which are sociological, economic or historical, then the teacher has only a limited scope for applying Maslow's theory to remedying the lack of motivation or inability to learn. In other words, it may have wider application as a diagnostic tool than as a remedial one. We shall come back to this point later in the chapter when we apply the theory to a real-life situation.

Let's have a look now at another commonly cited theory of learning: the Behaviourist model. The two famous names here are Watson (1931) and Skinner (1938). At its most simple level, their work has been taken to mean that we are motivated by reward or the avoidance of pain, and that the consequences of our actions or responses may lead us to change those actions or responses. For example, if I'm praised for attempting to answer a question, even if I get it wrong, I'll be more inclined to risk offering an answer the next time, too. If, on the other hand, the teacher just snaps 'No!' and goes on to ask someone else, I'll be less likely to risk the loss of face next time. Praise from the teacher is known, in behaviourist terms, as positive reinforcement. Positive reinforcement makes the recipient feel good, so they're more likely to repeat that behaviour so as to get that good feeling – that reward – again. This same dynamic can work in a less obvious and less positive way, too. If a student is being disruptive and, as a consequence, getting lots of attention from the teacher (even though the attention may be of the negative, 'Sit down and shut up' kind), that very attention may be seen as a pay-off and may therefore reinforce the disruptive behaviour. The thinking here is: 'Having the teacher shout at me is better than getting no attention at all.'

Learners who are moving towards the apex of Maslow's hierarchy, and are beginning to find that learning is a pleasure and a fulfilment in itself, will be moving towards becoming life-long learners, because, the behaviourists would say, learning is now providing its own reinforcement. But again, if we look at this theory of rewards and reinforcement in the light of Chapter 1, we see again that the task facing us is not always going to be easily solved at the level of the individual teacher in the individual classroom. The student coming into FE is likely to have already had at least eleven years' experience of education during which certain behaviours have been reinforced. If he or she has already learnt that one consequence of disruptive behaviour is that it helps avoid pain – that is, it avoids having to get down to work which may be painfully difficult or may painfully expose their lack of ability – then you, the teacher, will have years of reinforcement to undo. But you will have to undo it if you are to support the student's learning. And one way you can do that is by reinforcing positive behaviour and by removing the pay-off for negative behaviour. Removing the pay-off for negative behaviour is more easily said than done. In effect it means that you don't allow the student's disruptive behaviour to provide a way for them to avoid engaging with their learning. And that's a tall order. We'll see later in the chapter how it might work.

The third learning theory we're going to consider here is that of Rogers (1983), who is usually spoken of as belonging to the Humanist school of learning theorists. According to the humanists, the key factor in motivating student learning is the quality of the relationship between the learner and the teacher. Each learner must be respected and valued for who and what she is; and a relationship of trust must be built between the teacher and the learner. This is expressed by Rogers in the phrase 'unconditional positive regard'. The teacher should demonstrate unconditional positive regard for each learner, and in this way build a relationship in which learning can take place.

We can see at once how this theory relates on the one hand to Maslow's proposition, and on the other to ideas of the behaviourists. Genuine trust and respect from the teacher would dispose the student to feel safe and valued, and would be likely to raise her self-esteem. In terms of Maslow's hierarchy this would provide the conditions in which learning would be more likely to take place. And if the teacher is rewarding the student with trust and with respect just for being in a learning situation, then the behaviourists would agree that this would work very well as positive reinforcement. But what about a situation in which a student is behaving badly or disruptively? Wouldn't the 'positive regard' of the teacher in this context simply reinforce the undesirable behaviour? This is a good example to bear in mind in order to remind ourselves that the various learning theories do not always converge, and may even conflict. It is part of our function as professionals to weigh such theories against our own experience, and to decide what is useful to take from them and what is not.

Close focus

Can you identify any other ways in which the learning theories we have looked at might be considered to contradict one another? Take some time to think how each might apply to a specific incident from your own professional practice.

We are going to go on now to look at a 'real-life' incident faced by a newly-appointed teacher, and we are going to consider how he might formulate his response to this according to each of the learning theories outlined above. We are then going to ask ourselves whether there might be any other options open to him, or any advice we might want to give him. In other words, we are going to weigh the theory against a rather more pragmatic approach in order to identify strategies that could be of practical use to us.

Patrick

The journal entries below describe one teacher's experience of a student's challenging behaviour. This is a situation which builds up over time, and the student is one with whom the teacher has regular contact.

Task

When you have read this teacher's account, make some notes on how he might handle the situation if he were to base his strategy on what he knows about learning theory according to:

(a) ***Maslow***

(b) ***The Behaviourists***

(c) ***Rogers***

You'll find a discussion of his possible responses after the journal extracts.

Friday

Not a very good week. I was looking forward to working with the Return to Learning group, partly because they're all adults – most of them in their thirties – and partly because I think this is what FE should be all about. The sector of the second chance – all that stuff. People who've dropped out of education because it's part of their pattern of social deprivation. These are the people I want to help. This is what I'm in it for. But there's a woman in this group and I just know she's going to be trouble. She whines. I know that's not a very professional remark to make – but it's true. You'd think nobody else in the group has any problems, and you'd think all her problems were my fault. The teachers who made her feel bad at school; the people who design forms she can't understand. All my fault. At least, you'd think so. Anyway, today we were doing a session on letter writing, and she's not doing anything, not even picking up her pen, not even trying. So I say to her something like, 'Come on, Charmaine. This is useful stuff. You never know when you'll need it.' But she does this big laugh and says in her loud voice, 'No way! What do I want to write letters for when I've got a phone?' And she looks round at the others for support, and they just look back a bit warily. I think they're a bit scared of her (I know I am!). And I try to explain how a letter is sometimes more appropriate than the phone, but I'm thinking to myself that really I should be going around the room helping the others instead of giving so much time to her. But as soon as I move off to help someone else, she starts making a phone call on her mobile! Can you believe it?! So I go back to her and ask her to put it away and I remind her of our ground-rules. And the conversation goes like this:

'It's urgent.'

'Well, what's it about?'

'I'm not telling you.'

'Well, if you've got to make a call, why don't you go outside and make it?'

'You chucking me out?'

'No. I'm just saying —'

'That's effing charming, that is. I've got a sick kiddy at home and you want to chuck me out for —'

'I don't want to chuck you out —'

'Good. Right then.'

And she carries on making her call. Incredible! And there's no way that call was to a child. She was arranging to go out after college, and cackling like a demented chicken. And I'm sorry. I know that's unprofessional. But she makes me so angry, and there's nothing I can do about it. Never mind. At least it's the weekend.

Tuesday

The charming Charmaine again. How aptly named. Turns out she's been to see the Head of Department and told him I'm victimising her for being a single mother. Me! So Derek had me in for this chat, and there I was, having to defend myself. I think he believed me. He must have done, mustn't he? The irony is, she's the very type of student I came into this game to help. And I feel guilty enough anyway because I find her so irritating. And the knowledge that she wants to cause trouble for me makes me even less inclined to like her. And there she was in the class again this afternoon, watching me. And so I was exaggeratedly nice to her – smiled at her, asked her view on every topic (to which she replied indignantly every time, 'I dunno.'), and generally gritted my teeth and tried to be professional. About half way through the lesson, lo and behold! She gets her phone out and starts making a call. I look at her and she holds my gaze with this triumphant look, like she was saying, 'Go on, just try it. You daren't, dare you? Because I've got you now, and you know it.'

I just let it go. If she wants to play games, she can play them on her own.

Friday

Well, I think I've just about reached rock bottom, now. The lovely Charmaine has been to see Derek again, and told him that I'm ignoring her. I'm helping everyone else, apparently, but not giving her any help at all. Correct. Spot on. Because she's not doing any work. So what am I supposed to help her with? Am I supposed to spend half the lesson pleading with her to do some work, just to help her fill in the time between phone calls? I said to Derek, I'm there to help the students who want to learn (never thought I'd hear myself saying something like that). And he said, no. He said we've a responsibility to support the learning of all our students. So there we are. I can now consider myself well and truly told off. Thanks, Charmaine.

The question is, what can I do? I've got to turn this around somehow.

Discussion

If Patrick turned to our theorists for some ideas, these are the sort of analyses and strategies he might come up with.

MASLOW

Basing his analysis on Maslow, he might decide that what was probably hampering Charmaine's motivation to learn was a very low sense of self-esteem or a sense of insecurity about being in the classroom situation, or probably both; the one leading to the other. If she feels unsafe in the classroom and lacks confidence in her own abilities, these factors will act as barriers to her learning. Until she feels relatively safe and confident she will resist any encouragement to learn. According to this interpretation, her phone calls and her complaints are either avoidance devices or efforts to raise her own self-esteem by making herself feel empowered, or both of these. So, how can Patrick use this theory to inform his practice? Well, he could try to reassure Charmaine that she is welcome. He could try to make her feel valued. He could praise any efforts she makes in order to raise her sense of self-worth. But in practical terms what does this really mean? He seems to have tried the first two, but got little response

> *And so I was exaggeratedly nice to her – smiled at her, asked her view on every topic (to which she replied indignantly every time, 'I dunno.')*

And how is he to try the third if she makes no effort and produces no work for him to praise? The theory, therefore, may be quite useful in helping Patrick to understand why Charmaine is behaving as she is, and it will provide general pointers towards how to put things right; but in this case there's no obvious practical solution to be found here.

BEHAVIOURISTS

Basing his analysis on the behaviourists, Patrick might find himself even more disheartened. Charmaine's unco-operative and confrontational behaviour has already yielded her several rewards. Her aggressive attitude has, as far she's concerned, won her the right to make phone calls in class. Her complaints to the HoD have been rewarded by putting her in a position where the teacher is nervous of challenging her if she refuses to work or to abide by the rules. In other words, her bad behaviour has really paid off for her. She has learnt that it works. She's learnt that it gets her what she wants. Now, the sensible strategy for Patrick, obviously, is to apply behaviourist theory to encourage her to learn that such behaviour *doesn't* pay, and that learning and co-operation can be even more rewarding than argument and non-co-operation. Everyone, I'm sure, would agree that this makes absolute sense. But how does he go about this in practical terms, given the situation he finds himself in? He could praise every sign of co-operation; but so far there appears to have been none. He could with-hold reward when her behaviour falls outside acceptable parameters – or could he? Already she has complained about him denying her his attention:

The lovely Charmaine has been to see Derek again, and told him that I'm ignoring her. I'm helping everyone else, apparently, but not giving her any help at all.

Again, the theory proves useful as a diagnostic tool, but doesn't necessarily provide the necessary guidance on a practical level as to what Patrick can do next.

ROGERS

Basing his analysis on Rogers' humanist approach, Patrick might come to the conclusion that what is holding Charmaine back is a lack of trust in the teacher–student relationship. She doesn't feel unconditionally valued and accepted, and therefore is not motivated to learn. So, what's Patrick going to do about that? Here we come up against one of the problems with Rogers' 'unconditional positive regard'. It's not always possible to feel this for a student. In fact, it's quite clear from his journal that Patrick has come to actively dislike this particular student, and he is worried that this is somehow unprofessional of him. It would be unprofessional, I believe, if he were to make this dislike apparent. He is only human after all, and cannot control what he feels. But if he is sufficiently self-aware to be clear about what he is feeling – and his reflective journal will help him here – then he can make sure that this does not in any way affect the way he behaves towards this particular student. In other words, we may not always feel unconditional positive regard for our students, but we can behave towards them as though we do. And this can work, in terms of motivation. Think of Gloria in Chapter 5. When she acted as though she was enjoying teaching that particular class, the students began to respond to her more positively.

'Ah,' you might say, 'but wait a moment. I've read the earlier part of this chapter. If Patrick behaves towards Charmaine as though his positive regard for her is *unconditional*, how does that square with the behaviourist notion that he should only reward or reinforce her behaviour when it is acceptable or appropriate?' The answer is that it doesn't, really; and so Patrick, and you, and I, will always have to make a choice.

So, where does this all leave Patrick? He probably has a better idea now of why Charmaine is behaving in the way she is; but he may be no further forward in developing a strategy for motivating her or managing her behaviour.

Task

What would you advise Patrick to do? What strategy or strategies do you think might work, and why? You might like to jot down some notes on this, or record your reflections in your journal, before reading on.

Discussion

Patrick could use what he has learnt about the probable causes of Charmaine's behaviour in the following way. He could speak to her after the lesson. In view of the fact that she has already been telling lies about him, he would be wise to do this in a public space, and preferably with a witness. Another colleague or another student, or both, would be better than Derek the HoD, because having the latter there might lead Charmaine to believe that Patrick was only speaking to her under duress. If, however, she declines to speak with him, he will probably have to ask for a three-way meeting with Derek present.

Let's assume, though, that she agrees. This, then, is Patrick's opportunity to express concern that they have got off on the wrong foot; to tell her how much he admires her for returning to education; how he came into teaching just for the opportunity to teach students like her; that he would like to discover how she feels about the class and how he can best tailor it to meet her needs. From what we have read in his journal, we know all this to be perfectly true. And by saying it to Charmaine, and making sure she hears it, he is putting into practice some of the key points from the learning theory we've discussed. He is showing Charmaine that he values her as a learner and wants to establish a more positive and caring basis for their professional relationship; and he is emphasising the human to human – rather than teacher to student – nature of their interaction (Rogers). In this way he is, hopefully, making her feel more secure and raising her self-esteem (Maslow); and he is rewarding her co-operation (agreeing to talk with him) by giving her lots of validation – letting her hear positive things said about her (Behaviourists).

I think this is probably his best shot. It may not work immediately. He may have to do it more than once. In fact, he may have to do it several times. And each time he will have to swallow his irritation and his indignation, and make Charmaine feel that he means what he is saying. This is part of being a professional – the ability not to take things personally, or at least to behave as though you don't. Of course, it may never work, and at some point he will have to weigh up the needs of Charmaine against those of the other students and take the matter back to Derek the HoD and thrash things out. But first he has to try, because by not giving up straight away there's a possibility he may make a real difference to this student's future.

Close focus

If you disagree with this strategy, or if your suggested strategy is very different, take the opportunity to discuss this with a colleague or a mentor. Remember, there are no right answers. A strategy is only a solution if it works; and what works in one instance is not guaranteed to work in another.

Identifying your own theories of motivation and learning

One of the advantages of keeping a reflective journal is that you are able to identify, examine and test your own accumulation of propositional knowledge – the professional wisdom that you gain from your experience. This is what reflective practice and continuing professional development are about. You may, for example, already have encountered a student like Charmaine and discovered for yourself a means of motivating and engaging her. Whatever general principle you brought to bear in that instance, will, if it was successful, be the one you are most likely to apply if you encounter such a situation again. In this way you have come up with your own practice-based theory; and each time you apply it, you will be testing it and refining it, until you have a pretty good idea of when it will work and when it won't. But this testing and reflection is a continuous process. It isn't something that just finishes – for example when you get your Stage 3 qualification or when you've been teaching for five years. It is part of the on-going function of a professional to be theorising and testing that theory.

One way to begin to identify your personal theories about what motivates students and how they learn is to read factual or fictional accounts of teaching and learning and, first of all, to identify the theories which seem to underlie the practice, and then to judge the extent to which these coincide or conflict with your own. Even if you can only identify what you disagree with, this is a good place to start.

Task

Read the two passages below and decide

(a) ***what each implies about the teacher's theory of how to motivate students;***

(b) ***what each implies about the teacher's theory of what education is for;***

(c) ***the extent to which you agree or disagree with each.***

Passage 1

As I keep saying, let all the lessons of young people take the form of doing rather than talking; don't set them to learn things from books that they can learn from experience. It's ridiculous to try to give them practice in persuasive speaking when they have nothing to say, or to expect to make them feel in the classroom the power of passionate speaking or all the forcefulness of a good argument when they have nothing and nobody to persuade! All the rules of rhetoric are just a waste of words to those who do not know how to use them for their own purposes. What does it matter to a student to know how Hannibal encouraged his soldiers to cross the Alps? If instead of those great speeches you showed him how to talk his prefect into giving him a holiday, you can be certain he would pay more attention to your rules.

Jean-Jacques Rousseau: *Emile* (1772)

Passage 2

'This is the first class in English spelling and philosophy ... Now, then, where's the first boy?'

'Please, sir, he's cleaning the back parlour window,' said the temporary head of the philosophical class.

'So he is, to be sure,' rejoined Squeers. 'We go upon the practical mode of teaching, Nickleby; the regular education system. C-l-e-a-n, clean, verb active, to make bright, to scour. W-i-n, win, d-e-r, der, winder, a casement. When the boy knows this out of the book, he goes and does it. It's just the same principle as the use of the globes. Where's the second boy?'

'Please, sir, he's weeding the garden,' replied a small voice.

'To be sure,' said Squeers, by no means disconcerted. 'So he is. B-o-t, bot, t-i-n, tin, n-e-y, ney, bottiney, noun substantive, a knowledge of plants. When he has learnt that bottiney means a knowledge of plants, he goes and knows 'em. That's our system, Nickleby; what do you think of it?'

'It's a very useful one, at any rate,' answered Nicholas …

'Let any boy speak a word without leave,' said Mr Squeers mildly, 'and I'll take the skin off his back.'

This special proclamation had the desired effect, and a death-like silence immediately prevailed.

Charles Dickens: *Nickolas Nickleby* (1839)

Discussion

Passage 1

(a) What is implied about the teacher's theory of motivation? This was written a long time ago, but what the writer is suggesting here is something that still forms part of most debates about education today. He is arguing that the learner needs to see that what they are learning is useful *for their own purposes*. There's an important distinction to be made here between this and the idea of seeing their learning as being useful to society in general or to the economic well-being of that society. The theory of motivation that's being expounded here is that young people will be better motivated if they recognise that what they are learning is relevant to their immediate situation, and if they are encouraged to learn it by trying it out rather than just hearing about it.

(b) So what does this imply about what the writer thinks education is for? It would seem to follow from what we have just said that this writer believes education to be about the development of the individual, rather than, say, about serving some collective purpose such as building a better-educated workforce. We could perhaps make a link here to that liberal model of education that we encountered in Chapter 1: the idea that education should not be about fitting us for work, but about enabling each of us to fulfil our individual potential.

Close focus

Take a moment here to consider your own views about this. On an imaginary continuum, with education as a means of meeting the needs of the individual at one end and education as a means of meeting the needs of society and the economy at the other, what position best represents your point of view?

Education should serve the needs of...

The individual ⟵————————⟶ **Society**

Or would you want to argue, perhaps, that the need for fulfilling one's potential, and those collective socio-economic needs as defined by governments, will always coincide?

Passage 2

(a) What is implied about the teacher's theory of motivation?

Well, I think we could safely say that Mr Squeers subscribes to the Behaviourist school, although he applies the theory in a rather negative way.

> *'Let any boy speak a word without leave,' said Mr Squeers mildly, 'and I'll take the skin off his back.'*

He motivates by threat of punishment. The reward for obedience is to withhold the punishment. Remember, a central tenet of behaviourist thought is that we learn from the consequences of our actions. If, as a consequence of talking, we lose the skin from our backs, we'll pretty quickly learn to keep quiet.

(b) What's Mr Squeers' theory about what education is for? Well, Nicholas sums this up nicely:

> *'It's a very useful one, at any rate,' answered Nicholas.*

There's a joke here, but 160 years on, most of us will miss it. As we saw in Chapter 1, in Dickens' day the education of gentlemen was in grammar and the classical languages; but for the less elevated classes it was considered that an education should be 'useful'. There was much discussion of what constituted 'Useful Knowledge', and a great deal of mockery by progressive educators who came up with the scornful term 'Really Useful Knowledge'. As we know from Chapter 1, all this forms part of the origins of our current and on-going debate about academic *v.* vocational qualifications. Mr Squeers, however, takes 'usefulness' to new heights (or depths). His theory about learning seems to boil down to simply this: education is purely instrumental – a means to an end. The 'theory' – how to spell (or rather, how to mis-spell) 'window' is simply a device to lend respectability to what is, in effect, an undemanding, learning-by-doing, skills course, which – and this is presumably its most useful aspect – also gets Mr Squeers' windows cleaned and his garden weeded. Anyone feeling a little cynical about recent policies relating to training schemes or vocational routes through school might be tempted to read this passage as a metaphor for all that is undesirable about employer-led or workforce-oriented 'education'. Mr Squeers seems to believe that the 'usefulness' of what is learnt will itself justify the learning. But his theory leaves a major question unanswered, for who is to define what is and what is not 'useful' and what does and does not constitute 'education'? What seems certain is that Mr Squeers' definition does not involve learning being useful to the individual nor to any wider social purpose.

(c) How far do you agree or disagree with the theories implicit in this passage?

Hopefully, on reflection, you will find that your own views and theories do not entirely converge with Squeers'. If they do – well, that's one way of getting your windows clean.

Further reading

If you want a more detailed overview of learning theory than I have given here, you can find out more in, for example:

References

Armitage et al (1999) *Teaching and Training in Post-Compulsory Education.* Buckingham: OUP.
Kazdin, A. (2000) *Behaviour Modification in Applied Settings.* Chicago: Wadsworth
Maslow, A. (1987) *Motivation and Personality.* New York: Harper and Row
Rogers, C. (1983) *Freedom to Learn for the 80s.* Columbus, OH: Merrill
Walker, S. (1984) *Learning Theory and Behaviour Modification.* London: Methuen
Charles Dickens (1839) *Nicholas Nickleby*
Jean-Jacques Rousseau (1762) *Emile*

8 PUTTING THE FLAGS OUT

To change your mind and to follow one who sets you right
Is to be none the less the free agent that you were before.
Marcus Aurelius AD 121–180

This chapter looks at ways in which teachers can motivate students by helping them to recognise their own achievements, however small. It is about finding successes to celebrate and giving positive, constructive feedback, even in difficult circumstances. As well as examining the role that empathy and body language have to play in managing behaviour, it focuses on some of the attributes and qualities which the FENTO Standards set out as desirable in a good FE teacher, and explores how these might translate into practice.

The material in this chapter may be used for developing and reinforcing FENTO's list of qualities and attributes of a good teacher, as well as the following areas of skill and knowledge as set out in the FENTO Standards:

→ d1; d3; e4; f2; g1; g2; g3; h1; h2.

Leadership

The qualities which enable an individual to motivate and bring out the best in others are easy to recognise when we see them, but often difficult to define. If we can't define them, how do we go about fostering and developing them? This has raised the question in some minds as to whether the best teachers are born that way, or whether such skills can be taught. I think they *can* be taught; but I think that they can be best taught by example. I'm not sure anyone ever learnt to be an inspirational teacher by listening to a lecture on how to be one. One of the things we're going to do in this chapter, therefore, is to look at some examples of leadership, and see what we can learn from these about what it takes to give people confidence in themselves; to give them heart; to make them want to achieve. The first examples we'll look at will not be specifically from the world of teaching, but from other areas of leadership, because it will do us good to get out of the classroom and the workshop for a while. From these wider examples we'll be able to draw some lessons, which we can then apply to our practice as teachers, about just what it is that enables some people to bring out the best in others.

We have seen, in Chapter 1 and Chapter 2, that there are some students in FE who feel that there is no point in making an effort to learn because they'll gain nothing from it, however hard they try. We have also seen that there are some students who, for this reason or for some other, are uncooperative and mistrustful of you, the teacher. These are the students we want to reach; not just because it makes our life easier if they become willing learners, but because when we do reach them, and we do begin to find ways to encourage them and support their learning, we have the satisfaction of knowing we have done one of the most difficult and rewarding things a teacher can do. We have changed someone's life. We won't reach all of them, and we won't succeed every day, and perhaps not even every week; but we'll try to discover in this chapter what we can do to make this kind of success more likely.

To begin with, this is going to take us to Antarctica, and then into an open boat on the Pacific Ocean – a prospect that may come as a welcome to relief to some of us, after some of the classes we've taught this week.

In 1914 Ernest Shackleton set out with a hand-picked crew to cross the Antarctic continent – a journey of over two thousand miles. Their ship, the *Endurance*, became trapped in the Antarctic ice, which finally crushed and sank it. To get his men to safety, Shackleton led them for days across miles of disintegrating ice floes, dragging the small boats they had salvaged from the ship, and then across the open sea to the nearest dry land, Elephant Island, itself a barren, rocky waste. From there, Shackleton put to sea again in one of the little boats with a handful of the fitter men, and sailed 800 miles through the stormy seas of the South Atlantic to South Georgia from where he was able to organise a rescue. He wrote to his wife: 'Not a life lost, and we have been through hell.' His comment has become famous, summing up as it does the remarkable endurance and determination of this group of otherwise ordinary men.

Over a hundred years earlier history tells us of another, and in some ways similar, feat of leadership. This time the man in charge navigated a small open boat almost 4000 miles across the Pacific Ocean to land safely in Java without losing a single one of his eighteen men. They survived storms, starvation and attack from South Pacific Islanders; their leader took them through all of this to safety. However, he has gone down in history with a rather different reputation to that of Shackleton. His name was Captain Bligh, of the *Bounty*.

Shackleton brought his crew to safety, and in the process won their co-operation and respect. Bligh, too, brought his crew to safety, but in the process earned their loathing. They seem to have feared rather than respected him, and their co-operation was grudging, to say the least.

So, you may ask, what has this got to do with teaching in FE? My answer would be that it has a lot to do with it if we are interested in how people can be encouraged and motivated; and how mutinous behaviour or loss of hope can be turned into a sense of achievement and purposefulness.

It's tempting to imagine that the people Shackleton was leading were an homogenous, co-operative group, and that Bligh simply had the bad luck to find himself leading a surly crew. But this was not, in fact, the case. There were objections early on to Shackleton's plan to drag the boats across the ice, and some of the men, with the ship's carpenter as their spokesperson, came very close to mutiny. So how did Shackleton maintain his leadership and keep up the group's morale so that they remained motivated and task oriented? What were the differences in the way these two leaders behaved that produced such different responses in their crews?

Task

We'll have a look now at some of the things we know about how these two managed and motivated the groups in their charge. We can get some insight into this from accounts written at the time. For example, like you, Shackleton kept a journal. Bligh kept a log; and members of his crew recounted their version of events, too. Below you'll find some summaries of these accounts.

- ***Read through them and identify the conclusions we might draw about what kind of leadership behaviours are likely to motivate, and what leadership behaviours would tend to have the opposite effect.***
- ***How would you describe the difference between the attitude of each of these two leaders towards those in their care?***
- ***What links can you make here to classroom practice?***

When they first had to abandon ship and pitch tents on the ice in minus sixteen degrees, Shackleton tells us:

> *I mustered all hands and explained the position to them briefly and, I hope, clearly ... I stated that I propose to try to march with equipment across the ice ... I thanked the men for the steadiness and good morale they had shown in these trying circumstances, and told them I had no doubt that, provided they continued to work their utmost and to trust me, we will all reach safety in the end.*
>
> Shackleton (1999) p. 77

During the first few days cast adrift in the open boat, Bligh also made an attempt to keep up the spirits of the crew. The way he went about this was by telling them what it was going to be like when they reached the nearest land. Unfortunately, his stories of the savagery of the New Guinea inhabitants, far from entertaining the men, horrified them and made them extremely anxious.

As Shackleton leads the group across the ice, he reflects:

> *I knew how important it was to keep the men cheerful, and that the depression occasioned by our surroundings and our precarious position could to some extent be alleviated by increasing the rations ... The apathy which seemed to take possession of some of the men ... was soon dispelled. Parties were sent out daily in different directions to look for seals and penguins ... The possible number of permutations of*

seal meat were decidedly limited. The fact that the men did not know what [recipe] was coming gave them a sort of mental speculation, and the slightest variation was of great value.

Shackleton (1999) pp. 91–109

Bligh's crew in the open boat were similarly short of rations. They had all made an agreement at the outset to abide by the meagre portions that were necessary if their supplies were to last them long enough to reach land. Some time into the voyage, however, two of the crew noticed that Bligh, when he divided up the rations, kept extra for himself.

As Shackleton and his crew attempt to cross the open sea to Elephant Island in their little boats, he realises that the ocean's swell is moving them further away from their goal. He doesn't tell the whole truth to the crew, however, but simply says that progress is slower than they had hoped. And later, on reaching land, he allows the men to enjoy this achievement and get some rest before letting them know just how dangerous their situation still is.

When Bligh and his men make landfall on an uninhabited island to search for food, he is impatient to set off again. He wants to reach civilisation so that he can report the mutineers of the *Bounty* who have set them adrift. The crew want more time on land, to rest and find food. Bligh flies into a temper and screams at them. They should be grateful to him, he screams, because it's only his navigation skills that will get them to safety.

When the crew's carpenter challenges Shackleton's leadership, Shackleton tells him he will not allow one person's lack of co-operation to put the future of the rest in danger.

When Bligh's carpenter makes a similar challenge, Bligh attempts to fight it out with swords.

When the cook falls ill, Shackleton gives the task of cooking to one of the crew who seemed to have given up all hope and wanted only to lie down and die. He says:

The task of keeping the galley fire alight was both difficult and strenuous, and it took his thoughts away from the chances of immediate dissolution.

Shackleton (1999) p. 162

Bligh's crew, on the other hand, are made to feel useless. At every turn he reminds them that without him and his navigational skills they would have no hope of survival.

Bligh drives his crew to press on with their voyage because he is impatient to bring down revenge on the *Bounty* mutineers.

Shackleton drives his crew on because he knows that a sense of purpose and achievement are good for morale: He writes:

It will be much better for the men in general to feel that even though progress is slow, they are on their way to land, than it will be simply to sit down and wait for the tardy north-westerly drift to take us out of this cruel waste of ice.

Shackleton (1999) p. 82

Discussion

So what can we conclude from this about what kind of leadership behaviours are likely to motivate, and what leadership behaviours would tend to have the opposite effect? Taking the incidents one by one, these are some of the general points we might come up with.

Shackleton begins by praising his crew and expressing his trust in them and in a successful outcome. Bligh, on the other hand, inadvertently fills them with foreboding rather than with hope.

One motivates with praise and trust, the other instils fear about the future.

The way the two leaders utilise food is interesting. Shackleton sees it as a means of raising morale; Bligh sees it as something he must compete with his crew for. If we take food here, in the most basic terms, to be a reward, we see Shackleton using reward to motivate others, while Bligh seems to feel his own entitlement to reward supercedes that of his crew. This raises questions about the uses and abuses of power and about self-interest. It is also significant here that Shackleton sees the rations as a way to inject a small element of surprise and novelty into the daily routine. We might summarise all this thus.

One uses reward (food, novelty) to motivate the crew, while the other focuses on his own rewards.

Here we see something very similar. The issue here, too, is about goals and rewards. It is also about priorities. For Bligh, his own goal (reaching civilization and bringing the mutineers to justice) takes priority over the goals and aspirations of his crew, which are about regaining sufficient health and strength to make the rest of the voyage safely. There is something here, too, about expectations. Bligh expects gratitude and obedience, whereas Shackleton focuses on what his crew's expectations might be. Bligh also loses his temper – and quite spectacularly, too. This loss of control over his own behaviour is mirrored by his deteriorating control over the behaviour of others. We might summarise all this thus.

One leader focuses on the goals and expectations of his crew, while the other focuses largely on his own;

and

one maintains self-control, while the other doesn't.

Close focus

Shackleton keeps the whole truth from his crew. He doesn't let them know immediately how perilous their position still is. His reasoning is that they need to keep their spirits up in order to carry on. Is this justified, do you think? Translating this into classroom terms, would you ever feel it was justified to mislead students about, for example, the quality of their performance or the chances of their success, if by misleading them you might raise their performance or improve their chances?

In dealing with conflict the two again take very different approaches. Although both confront the troublemaker, Bligh chooses to escalate the situation into a fight. He adopts a position in which it is him alone in opposition to the crew. Shackleton, on the other hand, draws the lines very differently. He turns the situation into one in which it is he who is protecting the interests of the rest of the crew against the troublemaker.

The one leader adopts a 'me against them' position which escalates the confrontation, while the other adopts an 'us against him' position which defuses the situation.

Shackleton raises morale by making individuals feel useful. Bligh makes his crew feel useless by constantly reminding them that they are entirely dependent upon him to navigate them to safety. In this way he undermines morale.

One motivates by building others' self-esteem, and one demotivates by undermining it.

Intent upon his own goal and his own agenda, Bligh demonstrates no ability to imagine how the crew might be feeling and to take this into consideration. Shackleton, however, shows himself acutely aware of his crew's state of mind, and uses this awareness to inform his decision-making.

One behaves towards his crew with empathy; the other does not.

And so we now have the basis for describing two opposing styles of leadership behaviour. Let's move away from crews and ice and open boats, and let's talk about students and colleges and classrooms. In the context of teaching and learning we might call these two styles the Shackleton model and the Bligh model of motivation and classroom management. Set out side by side, they would look something like this.

Shackleton model	Bligh model
Motivates with praise and trust	Instils fear for the future
Rewards students to motivate them	Looks only for own reward
Focuses on the goals and expectations of students	Focuses on own goals
Manages own behaviour effectively	Loses self-control e.g. loses temper
Builds up students' self-esteem	Undermines students' self-esteem
Behaves towards students with empathy	Behaves insensitively towards students

How would you describe the difference between the attitude of each of these two leaders towards those in their charge?

With these two models of classroom management now clearly set out we can more easily see what it is about the attitudes of the two leaders which made them have such different effects on their crew. Shackleton's actions and decisions seem to be motivated by his care for others. Bligh's, on the other hand, don't appear to take others into account much at all. Shackleton is concerned not only with the physical welfare of his men, but also for their state of mind. Bligh doesn't seem able or willing to take others' feelings into account. Now of course we may be doing Captain Bligh a grave disservice here. For all we know he may have been a perfectly pleasant and sensitive sort of bloke, who just couldn't cope in a crisis. History is notoriously unreliable on these matters. But it's handy for our present purposes – and more fun – if we take history at face value and continue to use him as our model of what not to do.

The Shackleton model of motivation and classroom management, as we've set it out here, could be said to be based upon what Goleman (1996) calls 'emotional intelligence'. Emotional intelligence, put very simply, is an ability to take others' feelings and sensitivities into account, or to be able to imagine yourself in someone else's shoes. If we can do this – if we can imagine what our students may be feeling, if we can see things for a moment from their point of view – we can use this to inform our interactions with them. If we take the time to realise, for example, that they might be feeling unequal to the demands of the course, we may well put a very different interpretation on their failure to hand work in on time, or on their persistent time-wasting in class. We can see Shackleton using his emotional intelligence all the time. This man is losing heart – give him a task that concentrates his mind; these are afraid their efforts will fail – remind them of their strengths and make them feel good about themselves. And we can also see quite clearly how Bligh fails altogether to do this. He tells scary stories of cannibalism to men cast adrift in an open boat; he loses his temper and picks fights with men who are dependent upon him for reaching safety. How sensitive – how emotionally intelligent – is that? If we can take a moment to imagine ourselves in our students' shoes we are likely to gain a much clearer idea of how best to motivate them and gain their co-operation.

Celebrating success

Looking at explorers stranded on the ice and castaways lost at sea may seem a strange way to approach issues about classroom practice. But these are people who are in danger of losing their hope; and we have seen already how loss of hope may be an important factor in some of our students' reluctance to engage with learning. One of the ways we can motivate those who feel they have little to hope for from education and training is to find successes – however minor – to celebrate. This is another difference between the Shackleton model and Bligh model: Shackleton finds things to praise and celebrate – the men's courage, for example, or a tiny variation in diet – while Bligh finds things to criticise and feel fearful of. The Shackleton model of motivation and classroom management involves, among other things, putting the flags out. This doesn't mean giving undeserved praise. Sometimes criticism is necessary. But we don't have to do it Bligh's way. We can do it the emotionally intelligent way by using what Goleman (1996) refers to as the 'artful critique' (pp. 153–54). This means that the feedback we give focuses on what *has* been achieved and what *could* be achieved, rather than on what has not been achieved. In this way we are able to give some credit for any effort made, and any achievement, however small, and we are able at the same time to describe clearly what still needs to be done. Good teachers have been doing this for a long time. The name we would give it would be 'accurate, helpful and constructive feedback'.

So what links can we make here to classroom practice?

You'll probably have come up with some examples here of your own experience, as a teacher, or as a colleague observing someone else's class, or as a student yourself, when you have seen one or other of these models in practice. Let's have a bit of fun now, and look at how a modern proponent of the Bligh model might go about tackling the problem of unmotivated FE students. We'll call her Billie Bligh and we'll see how she handles a situation in which Jewell, a student, has repeatedly failed to hand in any coursework.

Close focus

See if you can identify the key characteristics of the Bligh model at work here.

Billie: *OK. That's it. You can all clear off. Not you, Jewell. You come here. I want a word with you.*

Jewell: *What?*

Billie: *Where's your assignment?*

Jewell: *I haven't got it. I've got to go—*

Billie: *You leave this room before I've finished what I've got to say to you and there's going to be trouble.*

Jewell: *What? You can't do nothing to me.*

Billie: *That's what you think, is it?*

Jewell: *Go on, then. What can you do to me?*

Billie: *Where's your assignment?*

Jewell: *I've told you. I haven't done it.*

Billie: *You haven't done it. Why haven't you done it?*

Jewell: *Because it's boring.*

Billie: *Not as boring as being on the dole all your life. Is that what you want? Is that what you're after? Because that's what you're heading for. Never affording a decent place to live, or a car, or a holiday, or any of that. Just daytime TV and—*

Jewell: *Well that's good, then, innit, because I like daytime TV.*

Billie: *Well that doesn't surprise me a bit. And it's a good thing you do. Because if you're not going to do any work you're going to fail this course and you're not going to get a job and you're going to spend all your miserable life watching daytime TV.*

Jewell: *Ah, piss off.*

Billie: *What did you say?*

Jewell: *I'm going.*

Billie: *Come here!*

Jewell: *I said I'm going. What you going to do about it?*

Billie: *I'll tell you what I'm going to do about it—*

(But Jewell has gone.)

Discussion

Well, all the Bligh ingredients are there, aren't they? Billie handles this:

✗ in a manner likely to escalate the conflict 'That's what you think, is it?';

✗ aggressively 'all your miserable life';

✗ confrontationally 'You come here. I want a word with you';

✗ using fear as a motivator— 'and there's going to be trouble';

✗ by undermining self-esteem 'being on the dole all your life';

✗ using criticism but no praise 'Well that doesn't surprise me a bit'.

We'll have a look now at how Tina Shackleton would handle the same situation, using – naturally – the Shackleton model of management and motivation.

Close focus

Again, see if you can identify the key characteristics of this model at work.

Tina: *Alright. Now, before you go – Listen a minute! – Before you go I just need to see one or two people for a quick word. Jewell, I'd like to see you first, now please. Don't worry, you won't miss your break. It'll only take a couple of minutes.*

Jewell: *What?*

Tina: *It's OK. I just need to talk to you about your assignment.*

Jewell: *I haven't done it, if that's what you're on about.*

Tina: *OK. Do you want to tell me why?*

Jewell: *No. Can I go?*

Tina: *Seriously, Jewell. I'd like to know.*

Jewell: *No point, is there?*

Tina: *Why do you say that?*

Jewell: *There isn't, is there. What's the point?*

Tina: *I don't know. I just think you'd be able to make a really good job of it if you gave it a try.*

Jewell: *Me? No way!*

Tina: *I think you're too modest.*

Jewell: *(Laughs) Oh yeah!*

Tina: *Yeah. I reckon you could do it. I bet you'd have some interesting things to say as well.*

Jewell: *If you could read it.*

Tina: *You'd be surprised what I can read. Unusual spelling, unusual handwriting. I've seen it all. Anyway, if you do it on the computer you can put the spellcheck on it. Give me it on disk and I can put the spellcheck on it.*

Jewell: *Teachers aren't supposed to need a spellcheck.*

Tina: *Don't you believe it. You going to do it for me then?*

Jewell: *Maybe.*

Tina: *Go on, then, or you'll miss your break.*

Discussion

This certainly looks more hopeful. One of the things we notice immediately is that Tina stops when she's winning. She gets a 'maybe' out of Jewell, and she doesn't press it any further. She clearly judges that she's made enough headway for now. Next time they talk about it she'll be starting from a much better position. Knowing when to stop is a good example of the use of emotional intelligence. Press it any further at this point and she could lose him. As it stands, she has managed in this interaction to communicate the following things to Jewell:

✓ She cares about his well-being 'Go on, then, or you'll miss your break';

✓ She is interested in him 'I bet you'd have some interesting things to say';

✓ She values what he has to say 'Seriously, Jewell. I'd like to know';

✓ She believes he is capable of meeting the demands of the course— 'I just think you'd be able to make a really good job of it';

✓ She won't be judgemental about his spelling or writing 'Unusual spelling, unusual handwriting. I've seen it all';

✓ She has a good opinion of him 'I think you're too modest';

✓ She is reasonable 'Don't worry, you won't miss your break';

✓ She has a sense of humour 'Don't you believe it'.

This is quite a lot to achieve in the space of one short dialogue, and Tina makes it look simple. But when we remind ourselves of the way Billie handles the same situation, we see how easy it would be to get it completely wrong.

Tina does some interesting things here. She defuses the potential confrontation by sidestepping the student's belligerence:

Jewell: *'I haven't done it, if that's what you're on about';*

Tina: *'OK. Do you want to tell me why?';*

Jewell: *'No. Can I go?';*

Tina: *'Seriously, Jewell. I'd like to know'.*

At the same time she is making the point that she cares. And she responds in an interesting way to the 'no point' argument. She doesn't try to persuade him that there is a point – in the sense that he intends – but instead she provides him with an alternative point, and that is that she would be interested in what he has to say. Instead of contradicting him, therefore, and possibly adding to his sense of grievance and inadequacy, she uses his negative, pessimistic comment 'What's the point?' as an opportunity to boost the student's self-esteem. We can also see her testing out an intuition that one of the reasons Jewell hasn't handed work in might be a self-consciousness about spelling or presentation. The way she approaches this shows a high degree of emotional intelligence. She refers to 'unusual' spelling. She makes no value judgement about it; and she also treats it humorously. In this way she raises the issue and at the same time defuses it, so that the student will be clear that there is nothing to fear here.

If we had to sum up here the difference between these two approaches – the difference between Billie and Tina – we could say that Billie makes the student feel unvalued and afraid for the future, while Tina makes him feel valued and optimistic. It's Tina who puts the flags out.

Other attributes

Following this dialogue on the page, however, we won't see what is perhaps one of the most important aspects of teacher–student interaction. It is, of course, not only what you say, but how you say it that counts. We might call this managing by example. We began to get a glimpse of how this works in Chapter 5 when we followed Gloria into her two alternative futures. It works in two ways. Firstly, if we look again at the way Tina and Billie behave during the interaction, we can see that Tina – like Gloria in the first of her alternative scenarios – models the behaviour that she would wish the student to adopt. She is reasonable; she doesn't lose her temper; she sidesteps conflict and aggression; she uses her sense of humour; she behaves towards the student with respect; and she adopts an open, friendly manner. Now, if this is the way she wishes the student to act, what better method than demonstrating it for the student by her own behaviour? Billie, on the other hand, provides a rather unfortunate model of behaviour: aggressive, confrontational, and generally negative. Her method for encouraging appropriate behaviour would clearly be not 'do what I do', but only 'do what I say'.

The other aspect of interaction which it's impossible to replicate on the page is body language. And here, again, the same principle of modelling can apply. It is well-known among those who advise on interview techniques that any face-to-face interaction involves a certain amount of 'mirroring'; that is to say that one participant in an interaction may be affected by, and begin to mirror, the body language of another. If, for example, Tina adopts a relaxed, friendly body language – smiling, nodding, arms uncrossed – there is a good chance that these signals will, even if he's not consciously aware of it, make Jewell feel more relaxed and accepted and at ease, and, what is more, he himself will begin to mirror them. You can test this for yourself the next time an appropriate situation arises. Try nodding, almost imperceptibly, as you are talking to someone; and the chances are you'll find them mirroring this body language back to you – a very positive and affirmative thing to have happening in any meeting! On the other hand, if Billie folds her arms, or wags a finger, or scowls, the student is likely to mirror exactly that negative or aggressive body language back at her, thus escalating the sense of confrontation.

Summary

We have looked here at two opposing styles of classroom leadership, and illustrated how one is more effective in motivating students and managing difficult behaviour. We have also seen how the teacher can themselves provide a model of appropriate behaviour, and can use positive body language to improve teacher–student communication. What this chapter illustrates, too, I hope, is that we can learn some useful things about leadership and motivation without having to go to academic texts on the subject. We can encounter examples and ideas on which to reflect in the ordinary course of reading for pleasure, or watching television, or simply by keeping an eye open for what's going on around us.

Further reading

If you'd like to read more about Shackleton or Bligh, and their styles of leadership, some interesting books include:

Kennedy, G. (1989) *Captain Bligh: The Man and his Mutinies*. London: Duckworth Press
Lansing, A. (1994) *Endurance: Shackleton's Incredible Voyage*. NY: Carroll and Graf
Toohey, J. (1998) *Captain Bligh's Portable Nightmare*. London: Fourth Estate

References

Shackleton, E. (1999) *South: Journals of his Last Expedition to Antarctica*. London: Robson

9 TEACHERS TALKING

A teacher affects eternity; he can never tell where his influence stops.
Henry Adams, 1907

This chapter relates, in teachers' own words, some of the most difficult or confrontational incidents they have had to deal with. It analyses and evaluates the strategies they have used, and invites the reader to do the same. The aim of the chapter is to present the reader with a range of possible solutions to difficult situations.

The material in this chapter may be used for developing and reinforcing the following areas of skills and knowledge as set out in the FENTO Standards:

➔ b2; b3; c1; c2; c3; d1; d2; d3; e4;; f2; g1; g2; g3; h1; h2

It also addresses the personal skills and personal attributes listed by FENTO.

Introduction

The material in this chapter is based upon responses from one hundred teachers currently working in Further Education. One of the questions they were asked was: To what extent have you observed or encountered student behaviour in the classroom or workshop which has had a negative effect on other students' opportunity to learn? Over half the teachers replied that they encountered this often or even every day. Not one teacher was able to claim that they had never encountered such behaviour. It is important, therefore, to bear in mind, particularly if you are a new or inexperienced teacher, that it is not unusual to encounter disruptive student behaviour; nor is it a sign of failure on your part. All FE teachers will encounter it at some time or another; many will encounter it regularly. The professional issue for us as teachers is not whether it happens, but how to deal with it when it does, and how to minimise the likelihood of it happening again.

How do we define disruptive behaviour?

You'll notice that the question was about 'behaviour which has a negative effect on other students' ability to learn.' This is because if we asked a question about 'disruptive' behaviour, we would run into difficulties. 'Disruptive behaviour' could be interpreted in different ways. We all have different levels of tolerance. What you find disruptive, I might find simply a little lively. An illustration of this is the response of one teacher who, asked to give an example of behaviour which disrupted learning, responded with: 'Excessive talking and general disruption *but nothing of magnitude*' (my italics). Some of us might suggest that excessive talking and general disruption was of magnitude enough!

But by focusing on student learning, we go straight to the heart of the issue. Unacceptable or inappropriate student behaviour should not be defined according to whether you or I approve of it, or can tolerate it, but by whether it presents a barrier to student learning. Our role as teachers is to support student learning. *Anything which undermines student learning becomes a problem which we, as professionals, need to address.*

The most commonly cited examples of behaviour which disrupts learning were the following.

- Talking while the teacher talks and/or talking about things irrelevant to the lesson.
- Arriving late.
- Using or answering mobile phones.
- Distracting other students' attention.
- Complaining and refusing to work.
- Expressing boredom and lack of interest.

For some teachers, it seems, these kinds of behaviours have become such a normal part of their classroom experience that they take them for granted and simply try to work around them. But if they were to look at this behaviour through a different perspective – the eyes of a newcomer to the profession, for example – they would have to acknowledge that there's a sign here that all is not well. One new recruit to FE teaching who had been observing some more experienced colleagues reports that:

> *During my first week I observed teachers allowing students to come and go as they pleased, talk while they were talking and eat packets of crisps etc throughout the lesson.*

Another confides:

> *There certainly seems to be a leniency beyond any experience I have encountered.*

A question they both go on to reflect upon is: Why are the students there at all if their intention is not to learn and, in the process, to disrupt the learning of others? In Chapter 1 we looked at some possible answers to this question; in this final chapter we shall take a pragmatic approach and consider some strategies for dealing with such situations on a day-to-day basis. It is important to remember, however, that the underlying reasons for students behaving in this way may often originate with policies which are drawn up and implemented at a national, regional or institutional level. What we can do at the classroom level is to deal with immediate and specific situations. We can't affect trends of attitude and behaviour; only the policy-makers can do that. One teacher described this as 'Holding the fort from day to day while we wait for the cavalry to arrive and bring better times.' This may be how it feels sometimes; but there is nevertheless a professional satisfaction to be gained when we succeed in supporting student learning in the face of difficult circumstances.

Task

Let's go back to those recurrent disruptive behaviours listed above. What would you say they have in common? You may like to jot down a few notes before continuing to read on.

Discussion

Well, clearly the first thing they have in common is that, although they present difficulties for those students in the class who may want to learn, they are not in themselves, taken singly, particularly serious breaches of manners or of discipline. (Don't worry. We'll be coming to some of those later!) They are non-violent and non-confrontational. They all indicate a lack of commitment and lack of interest rather than a serious intention to cause trouble. They seem to indicate one of two things: either that the student is bored and unmotivated, or that they are hoping to avoid having to do work that may stretch them beyond what they consider to be their abilities. Looked at in this way, the behaviour presents problems which may be open to a number of solutions.

Common behaviour management strategies

Let's have a look now at some of the strategies our sample of teachers used. Here's a list of some of the ways teachers addressed the most commonly encountered disruption – students talking while the teacher is trying to speak to the class.

- Give informal warnings and initiate formal report procedures.
- Ignore it. I'm not empowered to rectify this.
- Plan more group-work, so that they get a chance to talk, and I get a chance to focus what they talk about.
- Allocate ten minutes at the start of each lesson to have a chat (informally chaired by me) which allows them to catch up on one another's news, TV programmes watched, etc. Then we get down to work.
- Frighten them by reminding them they've got unit tests to do.
- Ask them to stop talking.
- Reassure them by saying the lesson's nearly over and they'll be able to talk about whatever they like to whoever they like afterwards.

- Refuse to sign their EMA (Education Maintenance Award) forms.
- Ask them what the problem was.
- Just keep telling them to quieten down and get on with their work.
- Move the noisiest student as far away as possible from the rest, right at the front where I can see him.
- Stop talking and stare at the students involved. The others then tell them to shut up.
- Tell them they can't go for break until they've shut up and listened.
- Tackle them, loudly and aggressively. Make them jump.
- Just talk louder so the rest can hear me.
- Direct some of my questions at the noisy ones to try to draw them in.
- Report them to their personal tutor.
- Draw up some individual, achievable goals with them.
- Warn them and, if they persist, tell them to get out.
- Broke the next session up: input, then student activity; input, then student activity. That way they didn't have to listen for too long, and they had something to get actively involved in.
- Spoke to those concerned separately and reminded them of the ground-rules.
- Set a target for that student to achieve in that lesson.

Task

How would you evaluate each of these strategies? How would you estimate their chances of success? You may wish to discuss this with a colleague or a mentor, or you may find it useful as a starting point for a reflective entry in your journal.

Discussion

As that long list suggests, there are certainly plenty of strategies to try, and what works in one situation will not necessarily work in another. But in the process of evaluating these responses it is likely that you have come to some conclusions about the *kinds* of strategies that are most likely to be effective, and those which stand least chance of succeeding.

You may have noticed that the strategies listed there fall into two broad categories: those where the teacher *reacts* by trying to *impose* order – for example, 'Warn them, and if they persist, tell them to get out'; or 'Just talk louder so the rest can hear me'; and those where the teacher becomes *proactive* and takes steps to *create* order – for example, 'Plan more group-work, so that they get a chance to talk, and I get a chance to focus what they talk about'; or 'Allocate ten minutes at the start of each lesson to have a chat (informally chaired by me) which allows them to catch up on one another's news, TV programmes watched, etc. Then we get down to work'. One of the characteristics which distinguishes between these two is that the proactive, creative approach will normally involve some element of planning; while the reactive attempt to impose order is, as the word 'reactive' suggests, an immediate and perhaps unconsidered response to the unwanted behaviour. Another way to view this would be that the proactive, planned response is more likely to be the outcome of careful reflection on previous practice or observation, whilst the reactive approach may have involved no reflection at all.

Close focus

1. ***You may like to take some time to divide the list into two sub-groups:* imposing order *and* creating order *(you can compare your version with the lists at the end of this section).***
2. ***In the process of doing this, did you identify any strategies which don't fit clearly into either sub-group?***

Let's take just one of those strategies now and look at it in more detail.

> *Move the noisiest student as far away as possible from the rest, right at the front where I can see him.*

Essentially, this is a reactive attempt to impose order. We probably all recognise it. It is a measure quite often resorted to, and seems, on the face of it, to make perfect sense. It has, however, one serious flaw, which is this: if you move a noisy or attention-seeking student to the front of the classroom or workshop, you provide them with the perfect vantage point from which to continue 'entertaining' the rest of the students. They have only to turn in their seat, and they can meet the eyes of their entire audience. This is the worst possible place to position a disruptive student. It gives them the floor. It makes them a more effective rival for the class's attention. Certainly, they are now within your reach. But to what purpose? You can hardly use force to make them work; and although you may be able to see clearly whether they are on task or not, this is still not a strategy for supporting their learning. At least if you seat them at the back of the room, or the lab or workshop where it is not easy for the other students to see them and to have their attention distracted, the majority will be able to get on with their work, and the talkative student *may* fall relatively silent for want of an audience and get on with some work themselves.

Going back to our list of strategies, this is how I would subdivide them.

Imposing order

- Give informal warnings and initiate formal report procedures.
- Ask them to stop talking.
- Frighten them by reminding them they've got unit tests to do.
- Refuse to sign their EMA forms.
- Just keep telling them to quieten down and get on with their work.
- Move the noisiest student as far away as possible from the rest, right at the front where I can see him.
- Tell them they can't go for break until they've shut up and listened.
- Tackle them, loudly and aggressively. Make them jump.
- Just talk louder so the rest can hear me.
- Report them to their personal tutor.
- Warn them, and if they persist, tell them to get out.

Creating order

- Plan more group-work, so that they get a chance to talk, and I get a chance to focus what they talk about.
- Allocate ten minutes at the start of each lesson to have a chat (informally chaired by me) which allows them to catch up on one another's news, TV programmes watched, etc. Then we get down to work.
- Draw up some individual, achievable goals with them.
- Broke the next session up: input, then student activity; input, then student activity. That way they didn't have to listen for too long, and they had something to get actively involved in.
- Spoke to those concerned separately and reminded them of the ground-rules.
- Set a target for that student to achieve in that lesson.

Task

Which of these two groups of strategies do you think would be more effective in the long term, and why?

Discussion

I've left out the ones which I don't think sit neatly in either category. Let's just have a look at each of these briefly.

Ignore it. I'm not empowered to rectify this.

This presents like a strategy, but I would argue that it is simply avoidance or denial. As professional practitioners our business is to support student learning. If disruptive talk is preventing student learning, then what are we achieving by being in the classroom and doing nothing about it? We may as well present our lesson to an empty room. We may not be 'empowered to rectify' student disaffection in general, but we have undertaken to do our best to support these particular students' learning. Our professional values dictate that we should at least reflect on how best to do this.

Reassure them by saying the lesson's nearly over and they'll be able to talk about whatever they like to whoever they like afterwards.

Reassure them that the lesson's nearly over? They're not serving a custodial sentence. They're not at the dentist. If they need that sort of reassurance, perhaps the teacher would do better to reflect on how to plan a lesson that would make such reassurances unnecessary!

Direct some of my questions at the noisy ones to try to draw them in.

This strikes me as quite a good strategy. In that respect it is an exception to the 'Imposing order' list. It is a strategy which suggests some reflection.

Stop talking and stare at the students involved. The others then tell them to shut up.

The same applies to this. Of course, it depends on whether you can cultivate 'the look'! But the use of peer pressure to establish relative quiet will usually be more effective than the teacher trying to impose it on their own; and it steps outside the unproductive Teacher *v.* Students construct that we have already explored in earlier chapters.

More behaviour management strategies

We began by looking at some of the most commonly cited examples of disruptive behaviour. We'll go on now to look at some of the other kinds of challenging or confrontational situations described by our group of a hundred teachers; and we'll consider the strategies, both general and specific, which they used to deal with them.

Task

Read through the list below, and reflect on how you yourself might deal with each situation. Think this through carefully before proceeding to the next section where we find out what action was actually taken by the teachers concerned. You may like to note down your ideas in your reflective journal and then evaluate them against what these teachers have to say.

- ***Constant shouting across the classroom.***
- ***Turning on the gas taps in the laboratory.***
- ***Sporadic attendance and failure to hand in work.***

- ***Verbal abuse – being rude to the teacher.***
- ***A student started taking his clothes off.***
- ***Listening to music on headphones when they should be listening to the teacher or getting on with work.***
- ***Fighting with tools in the workshop.***
- ***Arguing with the teacher.***
- ***Running about the room – won't stay in their seats***

No. I'm pleased to say that this wasn't all happening in the same class. These behaviours are not quite so frequently reported as those in our first list; but most of these, I would argue, are more difficult to deal with and potentially more serious. We'll take them one by one, consider the teacher's response, and decide whether this was the best (or only) way of dealing with the situation.

Discussion

Constant shouting across the classroom.

Here's the strategy the teacher used:

I tried telling them to be quiet. I tried several times, but it had no effect. In the end I sat them all together, the ones who'd been shouting at each other. My thinking was: if they're going to talk to each other anyway I might as well make it possible for them to do it without disrupting the rest of the class. That particular crowd – four of them – didn't get anything done. But at least the rest of the students could hear themselves think now, and they got quite a lot done.

This is a very pragmatic approach. It seems to be based on some degree of reflection, and what it amounts to is a strategy of damage limitation – accepting that the four noisy ones won't work anyway, and giving up on them for the sake of the rest.

Close focus

PROFESSIONAL VALUES

Are there occasions, in your view, on which it is justified to give up on the minority in order to support the learning of the majority?

Turning the gas taps on in the laboratory.

Here's the strategy the teacher used.

I stopped the class. I sent one of the more sensible students to fetch the Section Head of Science from her office. I told her what had happened and I asked her to remove the students concerned. She did so. I then explained to the rest of the class the possible consequences of such irresponsible behaviour. Then we resumed the practical session.

The students' behaviour was not simply disruptive; it was extremely dangerous. The teacher was right to treat the incident very seriously. He was right to stop the class. He was right to have the students removed. Will they be allowed back in? Will he have to go through all this again? We just don't know. Certainly he was lucky in having his Section Head within summoning distance, and fortunate, too, that she removed the offending students. Not every teacher has this option under such circumstances. Did you notice how he used the incident as an opportunity to reinforce for the remaining students some important rules about Health and Safety?

Close focus

PROFESSIONAL VALUES

If the Section Head had not been willing or available to offer support, what would have been this teacher's best alternative course of action?

Sporadic attendance and failure to hand in work.

Here's the strategy the teacher used.

I chase them up all the time. I report them to their personal tutor. I email them at their college mailbox. It doesn't seem to make any difference. When they do turn up they're completely behind with everything and I have to go over old stuff with them and the others get bored. It's not fair on the ones who turn up regularly. And if I wasn't chasing assignments from the others, I'd have more time to spend giving feedback to those who do hand work in. It's not one or two. It's about a third of the class.

This teacher is so busy being reactive – chasing the students – that she probably feels she has no time for reflection. It might, however, be worth her while to get these students talking (once she does catch them!) in the hopes of discovering whether there is any way she could turn them into more regular attenders. There might be ways in which she could rethink her planning, for example, in order to include a wider range of teaching and learning strategies. On the other hand, this is post-compulsory education. And sporadic attendance and non-completion of coursework is a widespread phenomenon which, as we saw in Chapter 1, may arise from causes other than the teacher's classroom practice. This being the case, any strategy on the part of any one teacher will have a limited effect and will not be likely to address the underlying issues.

Close focus

PROFESSIONAL VALUES

How much effort should the teacher put in to chasing these students and their coursework? At what point is she justified in putting the more motivated students' interests first?

Verbal abuse – being rude to the teacher.

Here's the strategy the teacher used.

Sometimes I think it's OK to act like you haven't heard. Sometimes that's better than making an issue of it. But this time I couldn't really let it go because she used such foul language and it was obvious that everybody had heard. I rounded on her and said, 'What did you say?' With hindsight I can see that was a stupid thing to do, because then she got to say it again, and there were one or two sniggers but most of them looked quite shocked. I told her – and them – very firmly that she had overstepped the mark, that she'd gone beyond the boundary of what I found acceptable in my classroom. I didn't shout. I just said it very seriously into the shocked silence that followed her outburst. And I said I would need to speak to her seriously after the class, but I wasn't going to do it now, because it wouldn't be fair to the others if I let her babyish behaviour hold up the rest of the class. I did speak to her afterwards – though I had to follow her down the corridor to do it – and she hasn't re-offended. That was three weeks ago now.

Two things here. The teacher recognises his mistake in asking the student to repeat what she said. It's an easy mistake to make, though; and arises out of the initial shock of hearing something unacceptable: '*What* did you say?' However, the rest of his strategy looks sound and seems to have succeeded. You'll notice that, by announcing he'll speak to the student afterwards, he avoids causing an immediate escalation; and by emphasising the care and responsibility he feels towards the other students, he avoids the possibility of being typecast in the Teacher *v.* Students construct.

Close focus

PROFESSIONAL VALUES

The teacher suggests here that it's sometimes alright to turn a deaf ear to students' abuse and to offensive language. What reasons do you think he would give for this? Do you agree with him on this issue? Where would you draw the line between language you would ignore and language you would feel it necessary to confront and actively discourage?

A student started taking his clothes off.

Here's the strategy the teacher used.

This was a Basic Skills student who needed a very high level of learning support. I just don't think he realised it wasn't appropriate. I said to him, 'Don't do that. If you're too warm we'll open a window.' His jumper was already on the floor and he was trying to pull his shirt off over his head. The others in the group had all started giggling. There was no way I was going to get any work out of them until he settled down. He was well and truly stuck because he hadn't undone the buttons. I went over and pulled his shirt back down and drew his attention to [the learning support assistant] who'd just come in with one of the other students. This took his mind off the undressing game, fortunately.

One thing this teacher demonstrates to us is the importance of context when we are considering strategies to deal with difficult behaviour. In her view, this student wasn't trying to be difficult. He didn't realise that his behaviour was inappropriate. Nevertheless, he doesn't respond to a direct request to stop. The teacher therefore decides to distract him, to focus on something other than the undesirable behaviour. This is the aspect of her strategy that any of us might find useful in a variety of difficult classroom situations. Change the focus. It often works.

Close focus

PROFESSIONAL VALUES

If this had been a student on an AVCE Health and Social Care course, or on an HNC in Engineering, rather than on a Basic Skills with Supported Learning programme, would this behaviour have required a different response from the teacher? If you believe it would, what response would be appropriate, and why?

Listening to music on headphones when they should be listening to the teacher or getting on with work.

Here's the strategy the teacher used.

This used to happen all the time. You don't see it so much now. Now it's mobile phones. Sending text messages to each other. Anyway, I have these ground-rules about phones. Before we start a session I get them all to put their phones on their table where I can see them, and switch them off. So when I caught a couple of them listening to this tinny sounding music through headphones, I stopped the class, waited until everybody was looking eyes front, and then told them that headphones and personal CD players were in the same category as phones. On the table. Switched off. A few groans. But they did it. I think they're OK with rules as long as you're up front with them and apply them consistently.

This teacher is quite clear about what's acceptable in his classes and what's not. And he makes sure the students are, too. You might feel that not all students would be so co-operative, and you may be right. There are some general pointers, however, that we can usefully take from his strategy. He makes sure that he addresses the whole class when he reviews the rules, and he makes sure the whole class hears him. And he emphasises that these rules are an integral part of his classroom practice; in other words, his response to the headphones doesn't appear simply arbitrary and reactive, but rather as consistent with his expectations about classroom behaviour. This is an important point because it almost certainly has some bearing on the students' eventual compliance.

Close focus

PROFESSIONAL VALUES

Some teachers claim that they would have confiscated the CD players until the end of the session. What are your views on this? What is your college's policy? What do you believe would be the advantages and disadvantages of confiscation?

Fighting with tools in the workshop.

Here's the strategy the teacher used.

I sent the rest of the class through out of harm's way to the other workshop where Rizwan was teaching. Then I called the police on my mobile. Then I shouted at the two of them that I'd called the police. Then I called security. By the time security arrived (two of them) one bloke had thrown the chisel down and run off, and the other was busy kicking a piece of machinery. We calmed him down. He went off with security. The police arrived. Statements and all that. They caught up with the other bloke in the end. Needless to say, they were both chucked off the course.

This is a more serious incident than most of us will ever have to deal with. The teacher's strategy, however, is worth remembering. First he gets the rest of the students to safety; then he calls for assistance. He does not attempt to intervene physically and stop the fight. And he is quite correct in this, since any injury to either man, following his intervention, could quite possibly – even if unjustly – be blamed on him.

Close focus

PROFESSIONAL VALUES

This teacher took a number of sensible steps. Is there anything about the order they were taken in which you would want to change?

Task

The final two confrontational behaviours in our list are these:

- ***arguing with the teacher;***
- ***running about the room – won't stay in their seats.***

How would you deal with each of these? If you have already encountered this sort of behaviour, can you remember how you responded? How effective was your response?

Use your journal to outline a strategy – a contingency plan – for the next time these situations arise in one of your classes. You may find it useful to look back over some of the earlier chapters, particularly Chapters 4 and 5, to remind yourself of how other teachers have dealt with a similar challenge.

Can adult learners be confrontational too?

One of the questions our hundred teachers were asked was about the relationship between students' age and negative behaviour. It is often assumed that it is only the younger, 16–19 (and now perhaps 14–19), age group which presents a challenge to classroom management in FE. However, one third of the teachers who responded to this question replied that they had experienced or observed difficult or negative behaviour from adult learners (that is, those over 21) as well as from the younger (16–19) age group. Perhaps we should not be surprised by this. The policies and practices which impact on adult learners are much the same as those which affect students in their teens. And with adult learners, as we saw in Chapter 2, there may be added pressures, of time, of family or financial responsibilities and of anxieties about returning to education or training. Moreover, for the teacher, the idea of issuing rules to an adult learner, or challenging their behaviour or pulling them up on their language or attitude, may somehow be more complicated than if the learner was a sixteen-year-old. Whether this is right or wrong is not at issue here. What is important in our current context is that you may feel as though challenging behaviour from an adult is more difficult to deal with than challenging behaviour from a younger student, particularly if the adult in question is older than you are.

Our sample teachers were asked to describe how they would respond to the following situation. You are teaching a group of adults on an evening Access course. There are nineteen of them, aged between 22 and 60. You call the class to order so that you can introduce the topic for the lesson. All the students give you their attention, except for one middle-aged man who has a newspaper open and is holding it in front of him, obscuring his face and is still apparently reading it. You say, brightly, 'OK. Are we all ready?'

He still doesn't put his paper down. The other students are looking from you to him and him to you, and you begin to feel embarrassed. You say, 'Colin? Are you in there? Are you going to join us?'

He just grunts, and rattles the paper, and carries on reading.

What do you do next?

Teachers came up with a variety of responses to this situation. The most entertaining – but one we needn't take too seriously – was, 'Set fire to his newspaper.'

Task

Consider what your response to this situation would be.

What might you say?

What might you do?

For each suggestion you come up with, try to follow it through to its possible repercussions.

How might the student respond?

How might you make him feel?

What might the other students be thinking or feeling?

Conclusion

As with most situations in teaching, there is no one correct solution. The important thing is that you are able to recognise, and to avoid, the *wrong* solutions – the ones which will undermine student confidence or motivation; the ones which will make matters worse or place you, the teacher, in an impossible predicament. When you choose your path of action you need to be sure that it is not simply reactive, but that it is based on careful reflection and, above all, on a careful consideration of your own professional values.

INDEX